This journal belongs to

....

Daily Encouragement

3-MINUTE DEVOTIONS
for Women

JOURNAL

BARBOUR
PUBLISHING

Member of the
Evangelical Christian
Publishers Association

Printed in China.

Introduction

Most days we're seeking out a moment or two of inspiration and encouragement—a fresh breath of air for the lungs and soul.

Here is a collection of moments from the true Source of all inspiration and encouragement—God's Word. Within these pages you'll be guided through just-right-size readings you can experience in as few as three minutes:

Minute 1: Reflect on God's Word

Minute 2: Read real-life application and encouragement

Minute 3: Pray

These devotions aren't meant to be a replacement for digging deep into the Scriptures or for personal, in-depth quiet time. Instead, consider them a perfect jump-start to help you form a habit of spending time with God every day. Or add them to the time you're already spending with Him. Share these moments with friends, family, coworkers, and others you come in contact with every day. They're looking for inspiration and encouragement too.

Your word is a lamp to guide
my feet and a light for my path.
PSALM 119:105 NLT

God's Promises Bring Hope

"For I know the plans I have for you. . .plans to prosper you and not to harm you, plans to give you hope and a future."
JEREMIAH 29:11 NIV

The writer of the well-known hymn "It Is Well with My Soul" penned those words at the most grief-stricken time of his life after his wife and three children were tragically killed at sea. His undaunted faith remained because he believed in a God who was bigger than the tragedy he faced. God's promises gave him hope and encouragement. Despite your circumstances, God has a plan for you, one that will give you encouragement and hope and a brighter future.

Father, may I always say, "It is well with my soul," knowing Your promises are true and I can trust You no matter what.

Behind the Scenes

*Now faith is confidence in what we hope
for and assurance about what we do not see.*
HEBREWS 11:1 NIV

Be encouraged today that no matter what takes place in the nat-ural—what you see with your eyes—it doesn't have to be the final outcome of your situation. If you've asked God for something, then you can trust He is working out all the details behind the scenes.

What you see right now, how you feel, is not a picture of what your faith is producing. Your faith is active, and God is busy working to make all things come together and benefit you.

———————◆◆———————

*Heavenly Father, what I see today is not what I'm
going to get. Thank You for working behind the scenes
to bring about the very best for my life. Amen.*

Rock Solid

"Therefore everyone who hears these words of mine and puts them into practice is like a wise man who built his house on the rock. The rain came down, the streams rose, and the winds blew and beat against that house; yet it did not fall, because it had its foundation on the rock."

MATTHEW 7:24-25 NIV

Prepare for tomorrow's storms by laying a solid foundation today. Rain and wind are guaranteed to come. It is only a matter of time. We need to be ready. When our foundation is the Rock, Jesus Christ, we will find ourselves still standing when the storm has passed.

Rain will come. Winds will blow and beat hard against us. Yet, when our hope is in the Lord, we will not be destroyed. We will remain steadfast because our feet have been firmly planted. Stand upon the Rock today so that your tomorrows will be secure.

Dear Lord, help me build my foundation today upon You so I can remain steadfast in the storms of life. Amen.

A Matter of Priorities

To everything there is a season,
a time for every purpose under heaven.
ECCLESIASTES 3:1 NKJV

Only one thing in our lives never changes: God. When our world swirls and threatens to shift out of control, we can know God is never surprised, never caught off guard by anything that happens. Just as He guided David through dark nights and Joseph through his time in prison, God can show us a secure way through any difficulty. He can turn the roughest times to good. Just as He supported His servants in times past, He will always be with us, watching and loving.

Lord, help me remember Your love and guidance
when my life turns upside down. Grant me wisdom
for the journey and a hope for the future. Amen.

Daybreak

"As your days, so shall your strength be."

DEUTERONOMY 33:25 NKJV

There are times in life when we feel that the night season we're facing will last forever and a new morning will never come. For those particularly dark seasons of your life, you don't have to look to the east to find the morning star, but instead find that morning star in your heart. Allow the hope of God's goodness and love to rekindle faith. With the passing of the night, gather your strength and courage. A new day is dawning and with it new strength for the journey forward. All that God has promised will be fulfilled.

———————

Heavenly Father, help me to hold tightly to faith,
knowing in this situation that daybreak is on its way. Amen.

It's All Good

And we know that all things work together for good to them that love God, to them who are the called according to his purpose.

ROMANS 8:28 KJV

God can and does use all things in our lives for His good purpose. Remember Joseph in the cistern, Daniel in the lions' den, and Jesus on the cross? The Lord demonstrated His resurrection power in each of those cases. He does so in our lives as well. He brings forth beauty from ashes.

What are you facing that seems impossible? What situation appears hopeless? What circumstance is overwhelming you? Believe God's promise.

———•◦•———

Dear Lord, thank You that You work all things together for Your good purpose. May I trust You to fulfill Your purpose in my life. Amen.

The Gift of Encouragement

We have different gifts. . . .if it is to encourage,
then give encouragement.

ROMANS 12:6–8 NIV

Paul spoke of encouraging as a God-given desire to proclaim God's Word in such a way that it touches hearts to move them to receive the Gospel. Encouragement is a vital part to witnessing because encouragement is doused with God's love. For the believer, it stimulates our faith to produce a deeper commitment to Christ. It brings hope to the disheartened or defeated soul. It restores hope. How will you know your spiritual gift? Ask God and then follow the desires He places on your heart.

———————•◦•———————

Father, help me tune in to the needs of those
around me so that I might encourage them for
the Gospel's sake for Your glory and their good.

Pass It On!

After the usual readings from the books of Moses and the prophets, those in charge of the service sent them this message: "Brothers, if you have any word of encouragement for the people, come and give it."
ACTS 13:15 NLT

Encouragement brings hope. Have you ever received a word from someone that instantly lifted your spirit? Did you receive a bit of good news or something that diminished your negative outlook? Perhaps a particular conversation helped to bring your problems into perspective. Paul passed on encouragement and many benefitted. So the next time you're encouraged, pass it on! You may never know how your words or actions benefitted someone else.

———————

Lord, thank You for the wellspring of encouragement through Your holy Word.

A Bold Request

When they had crossed, Elijah said to Elisha, "Tell me,
what can I do for you before I am taken from you?" "Let me
inherit a double portion of your spirit," Elisha replied.
2 KINGS 2:9 NIV

What a bold request.

Elijah filled the role of leader, prophet, and miracle worker. Why would Elisha want the heavy responsibilities and difficulties involved in this type of work? He did not ask to have a larger ministry than Elijah—he was only asking to inherit what Elijah was leaving and to be able to carry it on.

What might God give us if we asked boldly for the impossible? God deeply desires to bless us. If our hearts line up with His will and we stay open to His call, He will surprise us. God takes the ordinary and through His power transforms our prayers into the extraordinary—even double-portion requests.

Bless me, Lord. When my heart aligns with Your will
and when I ask for the impossible, bless me. Show me
beyond my expectations that You are my God. Amen.

A Little Goes a Long Way

"The LORD our God has allowed a few
of us to survive as a remnant."
EZRA 9:8 NLT

Remnants. Useless by most standards, but God is in the business of using tiny slivers of what's left to do mighty things. Nehemiah rebuilt the fallen walls of Jerusalem with a remnant of Israel; Noah's three sons repopulated the earth after the flood; four slave boys—Daniel, Shadrach, Meshach, and Abednego—kept faith alive for an entire nation. When it feels as if bits and pieces are all that has survived of your hope, remember how much God can accomplish with remnants!

Father God, thank You for proving that there
is hope. . .even in the remnants! Amen.

Go for It!

*When everything was hopeless, Abraham believed anyway,
deciding to live. . .on what God said he would do.*
ROMANS 4:18 MSG

"You can't do that. It's impossible." Have you ever been told this? Or just thought it because of fear or a previous experience with failure? This world is full of those who discourage rather than encourage. If we believe them, we'll never do anything. But if we, like Abraham, believe that God has called us for a particular purpose, we'll go for it despite our track records. Past failure doesn't dictate future failure. If God wills it, He fulfills it.

———◆———

*Help me to have the faith of Abraham,
Father God. . .to believe anyway!*

Feel the Love

Long before he laid down earth's foundations,
he had us in mind, had settled on us as the focus
of his love, to be made whole and holy by his love.
EPHESIANS 1:4 MSG

Need a boost of hope today? Read this passage aloud, inserting your name for each "us." Wow! Doesn't that bring home the message of God's incredible, extravagant, customized love for you? I am the focus of His love, and I bask in the hope of healing, wholeness, and holiness His individualized attention brings. You too, dear sister, are His focus. Allow yourself to feel the love today.

———◦•◦———

Long before You laid down earth's foundations, You had me
in mind, had settled on me as the focus of Your love, to be
made whole and holy by Your love. Thank You, Jesus! Amen.

....
....
....
....
....
....
....
....
....

Trembling While Trusting

*And straightway the father of the child cried out, and said
with tears, Lord, I believe; help thou mine unbelief.*

MARK 9:24 KJV

When the Lord looks at us, what does He see? Do we trust Him
enough to be vulnerable? Are we willing to obey even when we are
afraid? Do we believe Him?

Do not be afraid to follow Him, and do not let your trembling
hold you back. Be willing to take a step of faith. If you are scared,
God understands and is compassionate and merciful. Fear does not
negate His love for you. Your faith will grow as you trust Him. Let's
trust even while trembling.

---

*Dear Lord, help my unbelief. Enable me to trust
You even though I may be trembling. Amen.*

God Is Doing Something New

*"See, I am doing a new thing! Now it springs up;
do you not perceive it? I am making a way in the
wilderness and streams in the wasteland."*

ISAIAH 43:19 NIV

Imagine that desert, dry and barren—with no hope of even a cactus flower to bloom—suddenly coming to life with bubbling pools of pure water. That is what God promises us. He is doing something new in our lives. He is making a path through what feels impassable, and He will command a stream to flow through the wilderness of our pasts, places where we had only known the wasteland of sin and a landscape of despair. Have faith and bring your empty buckets to the stream.

———————

*Father, thank You for Your provision, hope, and joy.
Without You, life is dry and hostile. Come into my life and
quench my thirst. You are the only One who can fulfill me. Amen.*

My Life

*I long for your salvation, LORD, and your law gives me delight.
Let me live that I may praise you, and may your laws sustain me.*
PSALM 119:174–175 NIV

Can you really do laundry to please God? Can you really go to work to please God? Can you really pay the bills and make dinner to please God? The answer is a resounding *yes!* Doing all the mundane tasks of everyday life with gratitude and praise in your heart for all that He has done for you is living a life of praise. As you worship God through your day-to-day life, He makes clear His plans, goals, and dreams for you.

*Dear Father, let me live my life to praise You.
Let that be my desire each day. Amen.*

Pour Out Prayers

*Trust in Him at all times, you people; pour out
your heart before Him; God is a refuge for us.*
PSALM 62:8 NKJV

The psalmist tells us to trust the Lord at all times and to pour out
our hearts to Him. There is nothing we think or feel that He does
not already know. He longs for us to come to Him, spilling out our
thoughts, needs, and desires. God invites us to an open-ended
conversation. He made us for relationship with Him. He never tires
of listening to His children.

The Lord is our helper. He is our refuge. He knows the solutions
to our problems and the wisdom we need for living each day.

———————•⊶•———————

*Lord, remind me of Your invitation to pour out my
problems to You. You are my refuge and my helper.
Help me to trust You with every detail of my life.*

Solitary Prayer

Come near to God and he will come near to you.
JAMES 4:8 NIV

Do you have a prayer closet?

Jesus warned against people praying in public with the intent to show others how pious they are. Instead, He advocated solitude. Jesus often went off by Himself to draw near to His Father and pray, and that is what He suggested in the passage from Matthew.

A secret room isn't necessary—rather a quiet place where one can be alone with God. Maybe your quiet place is your garden or the beach. It might be in the quiet of your own home when your husband and children are away. Wherever it is, enjoy some time alone with God. Draw near to Him in prayer, and He will draw near to you.

Dear God, when we meet in the quiet place,
allow me to breathe in Your presence. Amen.

I Lift My Eyes

I lift up my eyes to the mountains—where does my help come from?
My help comes from the LORD, the Maker of heaven and earth.
PSALM 121:1-2 NIV

Adulthood is a time when decisions can be the most crucial. Challenges, failures, doubts, and fears may cloud decisions and cripple us into inaction because the end result is unknown. Career paths, relationships, and financial decisions are only some of the areas that cause concern. In all of those things, and in all of life, we shouldn't keep our eyes fixed on the end result, and we shouldn't keep our heads down and simply plow through. Instead, we must lift our eyes to the Lord. If we fix our focus on Jesus, we will see He is prepared to lead and guide us through all of life's challenges.

Lord, I lift up my eyes to You. Please help me and guide
me down the path of life. Let me never become so
focused on my own goals or so busy about my work that
I forget to look to You, for You are my help. Amen.

Morning Orders

*"Have you ever given orders to the morning, or shown
the dawn its place, that it might take the earth by
the edges and shake the wicked out of it?"*

JOB 38:12–13 NIV

God poses many rhetorical questions, all to show the might and
wonder and mystery of the Almighty. In these words are some amazing ideas that really cause us to stop and consider who God is. And
that is what we should do, especially when we face our worst trials.
Stop and consider who God is. That no matter what happens, He
will not leave us. And that He alone has the answers for us.

*Thank You, God, for providing glimpses
of You in Your Word. Amen.*

Stillness

Be still, and know that I am God.
PSALM 46:10 NKJV

David wrote, "Meditate within your heart on your bed, and be still" (Psalm 4:4 NKJV). Many of us have lost the ability to meditate on God. We either tell ourselves that meditation is something only Buddhist monks do, or else we cry out frantic prayers while distracted by the careening roller coaster of life. When we lie down in bed at night, instead of meditating calmly and trusting in God, we fret and toss and turn.

When we learn to trust that God can protect us and work out our problems, then we can lie down peacefully and sleep (Psalm 4:8). That same trust gives us the strength to face our days with confidence.

Dear God, quiet my mind. Remove from it all the worldly thoughts that come between You and me. Create stillness within me and turn my thoughts toward You. Amen.

Chosen

"I have chosen you and have not rejected you."
ISAIAH 41:9 NIV

The Lord doesn't dump us when we don't measure up. And He doesn't choose us one minute only to reject us a week later. We need not fear being deserted by our loving Father. He doesn't accept or reject us based on any arbitrary standards. He loves us with an everlasting love (Jeremiah 31:3). By His own mercy and design, "he hath made us accepted in the beloved" (Ephesians 1:6 KJV).

———————

*Father, thank You that I don't need
to fear Your rejection of me. Amen.*

Spirit-Oxygen

Tell me this one thing: How did you receive the Holy Spirit? Did you receive the Spirit by following the law? No, you received the Spirit because you heard the Good News and believed it.

GALATIANS 3:2 NCV

As we share the good news of Christ, we need to take care that we are not preaching the law rather than the love of Christ. The Spirit did not come into your heart through legalism and laws—and He won't reach others through you if that is your focus. Breathe deeply of grace, and let it spread from you to a world that is desperate for the oxygen of the Spirit.

Father, Son, and Holy Spirit, how grateful I am for the good news of the Gospel. Remind me of the grace I have received and enable me to share it freely with others. Amen.

Thy Will Be Done

He went away a second time and prayed, "My Father, if it is not possible for this cup to be taken away unless I drink it, may your will be done."

MATTHEW 26:42 NIV

Jesus didn't ask this once—He made this request three times in Matthew 26. These red-letter prayers reveal the 100 percent human side of Jesus.

In one of His darkest hours, Jesus was overwhelmed with trouble and sorrow. He asked God for something God would not provide. But Jesus, perfect and obedient, ended His prayers by saying, "*Your will be done.*"

When we face our darkest hours, will we follow Jesus' example? Can we submit to God's perfect will, focusing on how much He loves us—even when His will doesn't match ours?

I wonder why You refuse when I ask for what I think is right.
But Your knowledge is greater than my understanding.
So Thy will be done, God, Thy perfect will be done. Amen.

Valuable

*Better to be patient than powerful; better to
have self-control than to conquer a city.*

PROVERBS 16:32 NLT

Our world values visible power. We appreciate things like prestige
and skill, wealth and influence. But God looks at things differently.
From His perspective, the quiet, easily overlooked quality of patience
is far more valuable than any worldly power. Patience makes room
for others' needs and brokenness. Patience creates a space in our
lives for God's grace to flow through us.

———◆◆———

*Lord, when I come to Your Word, I am constantly reminded
that Your wisdom is not the world's wisdom. Give me Your
perspective. Draw me toward the practice of patience. Amen.*

Welcome Interruptions

So they left by boat for a quiet place,
where they could be alone.
MARK 6:32 NLT

Jesus and the disciples sought a quiet place, away from the crowds. Like us, they needed alone time. But as so often happens, people interrupt those moments of solitude. The crowd follows us, the phone rings, someone comes to the door. When that happens, we must ask Jesus for the grace to follow His example and let go of our quiet moments alone, welcoming the interruption with patience and love.

———◆———

Jesus, I am good at setting my own agenda.
Help me to see life's interruptions as gifts from You,
rather than disruptions to my "perfect" plan. Amen.

Right Now

For God says, "At just the right time, I heard you.
On the day of salvation, I helped you." Indeed, the
"right time" is now. Today is the day of salvation.
2 CORINTHIANS 6:2 NLT

God always meets us right now, in the present moment. We don't need to waste our time looking over our shoulders at the past, and we don't have to feel as though we need to reach some future moment before we can truly touch God. He is here now. Today, this very moment, is full of His grace.

Lord, make me mindful of Your presence right now, in this very minute. You have redeemed my past, and You hold my future in Your hands. This moment is the one I must cling to. Amen.

Satisfied

Satisfy us in the morning with your unfailing love,
that we may sing for joy and be glad all our days.
PSALM 90:14 NIV

God wants to fulfill you. He wants you to feel satisfied with life so you will catch yourself humming or singing His praises all day long. Even when life is hard, He is waiting to comfort you with His unfailing love so that gladness will creep over your heart once more.

———•◦•———

Father, You are the Author of joy. Thank You so much
for Your unfailing love that fills me to the brim. Give me
grace and gladness every minute of every day. Amen.

A Quiet Pace

"Teach me, and I will be quiet."

JOB 6:24 NCV

Do you ever feel as though you simply can't sit still? That your thoughts are swirling so fast that you can't stop them? That you're so busy, so stressed, so hurried that you have to run, run, run? Take a breath. Open your heart to God. Allow Him to quiet your frantic mind. Ask Him to show you how you can begin again, this time walking to the quiet pace of His grace.

———•‖•———

Father, quietness does not always come easily. The frenetic pace of this world sucks me in. Fill my lungs with Your breath. Quiet me and help me to be still. Amen.

Life and Nourishment

"I, the LORD, am the one who answers your
prayers and watches over you. I am like a
green pine tree; your blessings come from me."

HOSEA 14:8 NCV

Think of it: God is like a tree growing at the center of your life! In the shade of this tree you find shelter. This tree is evergreen, with deep roots that draw up life and nourishment. Each one of life's daily blessings is the fruit of this tree. It is the source of all your life, all your joy, and all your being.

———————

Lord, how can I thank You for answering my prayers
and watching over me? I am grateful for Your many
blessings and for You, the Source of my being. Amen.

Adorned with Grace

Don't ever forget kindness and truth.
Wear them like a necklace.
PROVERBS 3:3 NCV

Kindness and truth are strands of the same necklace. You should not be so kind that you evade the truth, nor should you be so truthful that you wound others. Instead, adorn yourself with both strands of this necklace. Wear it with grace.

———————

Father, there exists such a perfect balance between kindness and truth. One without the other would not be enough. Give me grace to be kind and boldness to be truthful. Amen.

Redemption

Put your hope in the LORD, for with the LORD is
unfailing love and with him is full redemption.
PSALM 130:7 NIV

When God permits a redemption, or "buying back," of lost years and relationships, we get a black-and-white snapshot of the colorful mural of God's redemption of us in Christ. When we one day stand in His presence, we'll understand more clearly the marvelous scope of God's redeeming love.

In ways we cannot now begin to imagine.

In broken relationships we thought could never be restored.

———◆———

I praise You, Father, for Your awesome redemption.
Thank You that I've yet to see the scope of it all. Amen.

Just What We Need

God can pour on the blessings in astonishing ways so that you're ready for anything and everything, more than just ready to do what needs to be done.

2 CORINTHIANS 9:8 MSG

Blessings are God's grace visible to us in tangible form. Sometimes they are so small we nearly overlook them—the sun on our faces, the smile of a friend, or food on the table—but other times they amaze us. Day by day, God's grace makes us ready for whatever comes our way. He gives us exactly what we need.

God, the more I see Your blessings, the more they seem to pour out on me. Give me Your grace to receive and eyes to see Your goodness. Amen.

Our Rock and Savior

"The Lord lives! Praise be to my Rock!
Exalted be my God, the Rock, my Savior!"
2 SAMUEL 22:47 NIV

Throughout the Psalms we read that David not only worshipped and praised God, he also complained to Him, was honest with God about what he was feeling, and even admitted to being angry at God. Perhaps the most amazing thing about David, though, was his constant devotion and reliance on his Creator. Even though David is the powerful king of Israel, he praises God in 2 Samuel 22:47, calling Him his Rock and Savior. David knew God was alive, and he also knew he needed Him more than anything else in the world. It's the same for us today!

Dear Lord, You are my Rock and my Savior. You
are alive, and I praise You as God above all else.
Thank You for Your love and power. Amen.

First Priorities

For Wisdom is better than all the trappings of wealth;
nothing you could wish for holds a candle to her.

PROVERBS 8:11 MSG

What do you value most? You may know the answer you are "supposed" to give to that question, but you can tell the real answer by where your time and energy are focused. Do you spend most of your time working for and thinking about money and physical wealth, or do you make wisdom and grace your first priorities?

———————•◦•———————

Father, if I compare myself too much with others, I can easily
get caught in the trappings of wealth. Instead, turn my focus
to You and help me to make wisdom my goal. Amen.

Control

Put GOD in charge of your work,
then what you've planned will take place.
PROVERBS 16:3 MSG

If we're doing a job that is important to us, it is hard to let go of our control. Not only do we hate to trust someone else to take over, but we often don't want to trust God to take charge either. We want to do it all by ourselves. But the best-laid plans fall into nothing without God's help. What's more, as we rely on His grace, we no longer need to feel stressed or pressured! We can let Him take charge.

———————

God, the more I entrust my plans to You, the more
successful they will be. Give me the courage to
trust and the grace to rest in Your promise. Amen.

Planting

*"I planted the seed, Apollos watered it,
but God has been making it grow."*
1 CORINTHIANS 3:6 NIV

Have you ever hesitated to engage in a spiritual discussion with a person because you didn't know how he would take it or you felt like you didn't have the time required to build a relationship with him? Of course, in an ideal world we'd have time to sit and chat with everyone for days, and the coffee would be free. But the fact that our world isn't ideal should not prevent us from planting a seed. You just never know what might happen to it. And that makes for some exciting gardening.

———————•◦•———————

*Dear God, thank You for allowing me to work for
Your kingdom. Help me to plant more seeds. Amen.*

A Lovely Place

How lovely is your dwelling place, LORD Almighty!
PSALM 84:1 NIV

Imagine this: God considers your heart His home! It's the place where He dwells. And as a result, your heart is a lovely place, filled with the grace of the almighty God.

———◦◦———

O Lord Almighty, I humbly invite You into my heart's home. Fill it with Your loveliness so I can experience the comfort of Your presence and Your peace. Amen.

Truth

*"You will know the truth,
and the truth will set you free."*

JOHN 8:32 NLT

What lies do you believe about yourself? How might those lies be preventing you from experiencing God's plan for *your* life? The next time you're tempted to believe a lie, write it down. Then find a scripture passage that speaks truth over the situation. Write that scripture verse across the lie. Commit the truth to memory. Over time God's Word will transform your thinking, and you'll begin to believe the truth. Then something amazing will happen—you'll be set free.

———————————

*Father, thank You for the truth Your Word speaks about my life.
Open my eyes to the truth and help me to believe it. Amen.*

Peace Rules

And let the peace that comes from Christ rule in your hearts.
For as members of one body you are called to live in peace.
COLOSSIANS 3:15 NLT

Peace is a way of living our lives. It happens when we let Christ's peace into our lives to rule over our emotions, our doubts, and our worries, and then go one step more and let His peace control the way we live. Peace is God's gift of grace to us, but it is also the way to a graceful life, the path to harmony with the world around us.

———————

Jesus, what an amazing gift of peace that comes from You.
Thank You for leading me on the path of a graceful life. Amen.

Unfailing Love

*But I trust in your unfailing love. I will
rejoice because you have rescued me.*
PSALM 13:5 NLT

Have you ever done that exercise in trust where you fall backward into another person's arms? It's hard to let yourself drop, trusting that the other person will catch you. The decision to let yourself fall is not an emotion that sweeps over you. It's just something you have to do, despite your fear. In the same way, we commit ourselves to God's unfailing love, finding new joy each time His arms keep us from falling.

———————

*Father, You have shown me time and time again that I can
trust You because You have consistently rescued me with Your
unfailing love. I commit myself to Your loving arms. Amen.*

Blessing Others

"Bless those who curse you. Pray for those who hurt you."
LUKE 6:28 NLT

Not only does God bless us, but we are called to bless others. God wants to show the world His grace through us. He can do this when we show our commitment to make God's love real in the world around us through our words and actions, as well as through our prayer life. We offer blessings to others when we greet a scowl with a smile, when we refuse to respond to angry words, and when we offer understanding to those who are angry and hurt.

God, I sometimes forget that the world is watching. I long to shine Your light to everyone I see. Help me to bestow blessings on others, even when they hurt me. Amen.

Board God's Boat

Then, because so many people were coming and going that
they did not even have a chance to eat, he said to them, "Come
with me by yourselves-to a quiet place and get some rest."
MARK 6:31-32 NIV

The apostles ministered tirelessly—so much so, they had little time to
eat. As they gathered around Jesus to report their activities, the Lord
noticed they had neglected to take time for themselves. Sensitive to
their needs, the Savior instructed them to retreat by boat with Him
to a solitary place of rest where He was able to minister to them.

Often we allow the hectic pace of daily life to drain us physically
and spiritually, and in the process, we deny ourselves time alone to
pray and read God's Word. Meanwhile, God patiently waits.

So perhaps it's time to board God's boat to a quieter place and
not jump ship!

Heavenly Father, in my hectic life I've neglected time apart
with You. Help me to board Your boat and stay afloat
through spending time in Your Word and in prayer. Amen.

Do a Little Dance

Then Miriam. . .took a tambourine and led all the women as they played their tambourines and danced.
EXODUS 15:20 NLT

Can you imagine the enormous celebration that broke out among the children of Israel when God miraculously saved them from Pharaoh's army? Even dignified prophetess Miriam grabbed her tambourine and cut loose with her girlfriends. Despite adverse circumstances, she heard God's music and did His dance. Isn't that our goal today? To hear God's music above the world's cacophony and do His dance as we recognize everyday miracles in our lives?

Make me aware of Your everyday miracles, Father. Help me listen closely for Your music so I can join in the dance. Amen.

Quiet Grace

Patient persistence pierces through indifference;
gentle speech breaks down rigid defenses.
PROVERBS 25:15 MSG

When we're in the midst of an argument, we often become fixated on winning. We turn conflicts into power struggles, and we want to come out the victor. By sheer force, if necessary, we want to shape people to our will. But that is not the way God treats us. His grace is gentle and patient rather than loud and forceful. We need to follow His example and let His quiet grace speak through us in His timing rather than ours.

———————

Father, thank You for the gentleness of Your grace. Give me a
spirit of patient persistence. Instill my words with gentleness.
May I always value relationships over being right. Amen.

When Words Fail Me

Before a word is on my tongue you,
LORD, know it completely.

PSALM 139:4 NIV

Sometimes Christians feel so overwhelmed by their needs or by the greatness of God that they simply can't pray. When the words won't come, God helps to create them. Paul says in Romans 8:26 (NLT), "And the Holy Spirit helps us in our weakness. For example, we don't know what God wants us to pray for. But the Holy Spirit prays for us with groanings that cannot be expressed in words."

God hears your prayers even before you pray them. When you don't know what to say and the words won't come, you can simply ask God to help you by praying on your behalf.

Dear God, I'm grateful today that in
my silence You still hear me. Amen.

Our Song

By day the LORD directs his love, at night his song
is with me—a prayer to the God of my life.
PSALM 42:8 NIV

All through the Bible, we find people worshipping God through song. They sing to God about winning battles and the birth of babies. They sing songs of lament and songs of praise, songs sinking with sorrow and songs bouncing with joy. There is, of course, a whole book devoted just to this practice: Psalms. . . . By day God guides us, and at night He still leaves the doors of communication open. What do you think His song is saying to you? What do you want to sing to Him?

———————

Dear God, help me listen for Your song and help me
find the words to sing praise to You every day. Amen.

Simply Happy

Are any of you happy? You should sing praises.
JAMES 5:13 NLT

Some days are simply happy days. The sun shines, people make us laugh, and life seems good. A day like that is a special grace. Thank God for it. As you hum through your day, don't forget to sing His praises.

———————•:•———————

Father, thank You for the gift of happiness and for life in the Holy Spirit that allows me to sing praises through my days. I praise You with all my heart. Amen.

"Extended" Family

God sets the lonely in families.
PSALM 68:6 NIV

God knows we need others. We need their love and support, their understanding, and their simple physical presence nearby. That is why He gives us families. Families don't need to be related by blood though. They might be the people you work with or the people you go to church with or the group of friends you've known since grade school. Whoever they are, they're the people who make God's grace real to you every day.

———•❧•———

Father, thank You for creating me with a longing for connection. Thank You for those You have placed in my life to make me more of who You created me to be. Amen.

Choose Grace

*And a servant of the Lord must not quarrel but must
be kind to everyone, a good teacher, and patient.*

2 TIMOTHY 2:24 NCV

Some days we can't help but feel irritated and out of sorts. But no matter how we feel on the inside, we can choose our outward behavior. We can make the decision to let disagreements go, to refuse to argue, to act in kindness, to show patience and a willingness to listen (even when we feel impatient). We can choose to walk in grace.

*Lord, help me be kind to everyone, to be a good teacher,
and to be patient with others. Thank You for Your
grace that allows me to be Your servant. Amen.*

Fear and Dread

What I feared has come upon me;
what I dreaded has happened to me.

JOB 3:25 NIV

Do we have a secret fear or dread? God knew Job's secret fears but still called him "blameless and upright" (Job 1:8 NIV). God doesn't withhold His love if we harbor unspoken dread. He doesn't love us any less because of secret anxieties. The Lord "is like a father to his children. . . .he remembers we are only dust" (Psalm 103:13–14 NLT). God never condemned Job (and He'll never condemn us) for private fears. He encourages us, as He did Job, to trust Him. He alone retains control over all creation and all circumstances (Job 38–41).

Father, please stay beside me when
what I dread most comes to me. Amen.

Simply Love

*But I am giving you a new command. You must
love each other, just as I have loved you.*

JOHN 13:34 CEV

Christ doesn't ask us to point out others' faults. He doesn't require that we be the morality squad, focusing on all that is sinful in the world around us. Instead, He wants us simply to love, just as He loves us. When we do, the world will see God's grace shining in our lives.

*Jesus, there is such simplicity in merely loving others with
Your love. Help me to follow this new command and let
the world see Your grace shining in my life. Amen.*

The Secret of Serendipity

A happy heart makes the face cheerful.
PROVERBS 15:13 NIV

Can you remember the last time you laughed in wild abandon? Better yet, when was the last time you did something fun, outrageous, or out of the ordinary? Perhaps it is an activity you haven't done since you were a child, like slip down a waterslide, strap on a pair of ice skates, or pitch a tent and camp overnight. A happy heart turns life's situations into opportunities for fun. When we seek innocent pleasures, we glean the benefits of a happy heart. So try a bit of whimsy just for fun. And rediscover the secret of serendipity.

*Dear Lord, because of You, I have a happy heart. Lead me
to do something fun and spontaneous today! Amen.*

Mirror Image

Behold, thou art fair, my love; behold,
thou art fair; thou hast doves' eyes.
SONG OF SOLOMON 1:15 KJV

No matter how hard we try, when the focus is on self, we see short-comings. Our only hope is to see ourselves through a different mirror. We must remember that as we grow as Christians, we take on the characteristics of Christ. The more we become like Him, the more beautiful we are in our own eyes and to those around us. God loves to behold us when we are covered in Christ. The mirror image He sees has none of the blemishes or imperfections, only the beauty.

O God, thank You for beholding me as being fair and
valuable. Help me to see myself through Your eyes. Amen.

Radiant

*"If you are filled with light, with no dark
corners, then your whole life will be radiant,
as though a floodlight were filling you with light."*

LUKE 11:36 NLT

We all have dark corners in our lives that we keep hidden. We hide them from others. We hide them from God, and we even try to hide them from ourselves. But God wants to shine His light even into our darkest, most private nooks and crannies. He wants us to step out into the floodlight of His love—and then His grace will make us shine.

*Heavenly Father, fill me with light. Shine Your
radiance on all my dark corners. Remove my shame
and help me to bask in the light of Your love. Amen.*

Stop and Consider

*"Listen to this, Job; stop and consider God's wonders.
Do you know how God controls the clouds and makes his
lightning flash? Do you know how the clouds hang poised,
those wonders of him who has perfect knowledge?"*

JOB 37:14-16 NIV

"Stop and consider My wonders," God told Job. Then He pointed to ordinary observations of the natural world surrounding Job—the clouds that hung poised in the sky, the flashes of lightning. "Not so very ordinary" was God's lesson. Maybe He was trying to remind us there is no such thing as ordinary. Let's open our eyes and see the wonders around us.

———◦◦———

*O Father, teach me to stop and consider the ordinary moments
of my life as reminders of You. Help me not to overlook Your
daily care and provisions that surround my day. Amen.*

He Is Faithful

*If we are unfaithful, he remains
faithful, for he cannot deny who he is.*
2 TIMOTHY 2:13 NLT

Sometimes we treat our relationship with God the same as we do
with other people. We promise Him we'll start spending more time
with Him in prayer and Bible study. Soon the daily distractions of
life get in the way, and we're back in our same routine, minus prayer
and Bible study.

Even when we fail to live up to our expectations, our heavenly
Father doesn't pick up His judge's gavel and condemn us for unfaith-
fulness. Instead, He remains a faithful supporter, encouraging us to
keep trying to hold up our end of the bargain. Take comfort in His
faithfulness, and let that encourage you toward a deeper relationship with Him.

*Father, thank You for Your unending faithfulness. Every
day I fall short of Your standards, but You're always there,
encouraging me and lifting me up. Please help me to be more
faithful to You—in the big things and in the little things. Amen.*

Practicality vs. Passion

Leaving her water jar, the woman went back to the town and said to the people, "Come, see a man who told me everything I ever did. Could this be the Messiah?"

JOHN 4:28–29 NIV

Practicality gave way to passion the day the woman at the well abandoned her task, laid down her jar and ran into town. Everything changed the day she met a man at the well and He asked her for a drink of water. Although they had never met before, He told her everything she had ever done, and then He offered her living water that would never run dry. Do you live with such passion, or do you cling to your water jar? Has an encounter with Christ made an impact that cannot be denied in your life?

Lord, help me to lay down anything that stifles my passion for sharing the Good News with others. Amen.

Grounded in Love

*"You'll be built solid, grounded in righteousness,
far from any trouble—nothing to fear!"*
ISAIAH 54:12 MSG

Balance isn't something we can achieve in ourselves. Just when we think we have it all together, life has a tendency to come crashing down around our ears. But even in the midst of life's most chaotic moments, God gives us grace; He keeps us balanced in His love. Like a building that is built to sway in an earthquake without falling down, we will stay standing if we remain grounded in His love.

Heavenly Father, keep me grounded in Your love. Provide for me a strong foundation to keep me stable through life's most chaotic moments. Thank You for Your steady hand. Amen.

Chosen

"Before I formed you in the womb I knew you [and approved of you as My chosen instrument], and before you were born I consecrated you."

JEREMIAH 1:5 AMP

God said that before He formed Jeremiah in his mother's womb, He knew him. God separated him from everyone else to perform a specific task, and He consecrated him for that purpose. We can be sure that if God did that for Jeremiah, He did it for each one of us. Nothing about us or our circumstances surprises God. He knew about everything before we were born. And He ordained that we should walk in those ways because we are uniquely qualified by Him to do so. What an awesome God we serve!

———————◦•◦———————

Father, the thought that You chose me before the foundation of the world and set me apart for a specific calling is humbling. You are so good. May I go forward with a renewed purpose in life. Amen.

Mind, Body, Spirit. . .

*I stretch myself out. I sleep. Then I'm
up again—rested, tall and steady.*

PSALM 3:5 MSG

Rest is one of God's gifts to us, a gift we regularly need. In sleep, we are renewed, mind, body, and spirit. Don't turn away from this most natural and practical of gifts!

———◦•◦———

Father, the gift of sleep is a glorious thing. Help me not to resist this gift, and help me to recognize the necessity of being refreshed and renewed by hours of rest. Amen.

Refreshing Gift

*For we have great joy and consolation in your love, because
the hearts of the saints have been refreshed by you, brother.*
PHILEMON 7 NKJV

Jesus always took the time for those who reached out to Him. In a
crowd of people He stopped to help a woman who touched Him.
His quiet love extended to everyone who asked, whether verbally
or with unspoken need. God brings people into our path who need
our encouragement. We must consider those around us. Smile and
thank the waiter, the cashier, the people who help in small ways.
Cheering others can have the effect of an energizing drink of water
so they will be able to finish the race with a smile.

———————————◆◆———————————

*Jesus, thank You for being an example of how to
encourage and refresh others. Help me see their
need and be willing to reach out. Amen.*

Annual or Perennial?

They are like trees planted along the riverbank, bearing fruit each season. Their leaves never wither, and they prosper in all they do.

PSALM 1:3 NLT

Annuals or perennials? Each has its advantages. Annuals are inexpensive, provide instant gratification, and keep boredom from setting in. Perennials require an initial investment but, when properly tended, faithfully provide beauty year after year—long after the annuals have dried up and withered away. Perennials are designed for the long haul—not just short-term enjoyment, but long-term beauty. The application to our lives is twofold. First, be a perennial—long-lasting, enduring, slow growing, steady, and faithful. Second, don't be discouraged by your inevitable dormant seasons. Tend to your soul, and it will reward you with years of lush blossoms.

Father, be the gardener of my soul. Amen.

God in the Details

*"When we heard of it, our hearts melted in fear and
everyone's courage failed because of you, for the LORD
your God is God in heaven above and on the earth below."*
JOSHUA 2:11 NIV

Sometimes, when our lives seem to be under siege from the demands
of work, bills, family, whatever—finding the work of God amid the
strife can be difficult. Even though we acknowledge His power, we
may overlook the gentle touches, the small ways in which He makes
every day a little easier. Just as the Lord cares for the tiniest bird
(Matthew 10:29-31), so He seeks to be a part of every detail in your
life. Look for Him there.

*Father God, I know You are by my side every day, good or bad,
and that You love and care for me. Help me to see Your work
in my life and in the lives of my friends and family. Amen.*

Holding the Line

*When I said, "My foot is slipping," your unfailing love,
LORD, supported me. When anxiety was great
within me, your consolation brought me joy.*
PSALM 94:18–19 NIV

Often we may feel that our feet are slipping in life. We lose our grip. Anxiety becomes a sleep-robber, headache-giver, and joy-squelcher. Fear takes over our hearts. All we can think is, *Just get me out of here!* But we must remember who is anchoring our life. God's powerful grip secures us—even in the most difficult times. He comforts us with His loving presence that defies understanding. He provides wisdom to guide our steps through life's toughest challenges. We can rest assured that His support is steady, reliable, and motivated by His love for us.

*Jesus, my rock and fortress, thank You that Your strength
is made available to me. Steady me with the surety
of Your love. Replace my anxiety with peace and joy,
reflecting a life that's secured by the Almighty. Amen.*

Seeking an Oasis

*He changes a wilderness into a pool of water
and a dry land into springs of water.*
PSALM 107:35 NASB

The wilderness of Israel is truly a barren wasteland—nothing but rocks and parched sand stretching as far as the distant horizon. The life-and-death contrast between stark desert and pools of oasis water is startling. Our lives can feel parched too. Colorless. Devoid of life. But God has the power to transform desert lives into gurgling, spring-of-water lives. Ask Him to bubble up springs of hope within you today.

———————•◦•———————

When I am feeling parched, Jesus, I trust You'll create a peaceful oasis in my soul. Envelop my spirit in Your hope, Lord.

A New Tomorrow

Rahab the harlot. . .Joshua spared. . .for she hid the messengers whom Joshua sent to spy out Jericho.
JOSHUA 6:25 NASB

Rahab was the unlikeliest of heroes: a prostitute who sold her body in the darkest shadows. Yet she was the very person God chose to fulfill His prophecy. How astoundingly freeing! Especially for those of us ashamed of our past. God loved Rahab for who she was—not what she did. Rahab is proof that God can and will use anyone for His higher purposes. Anyone. Even you and me.

———————

When I feel absolutely useless, God, remind me of Rahab's story. If You could use Rahab for Your purposes, You can certainly use me!

Anxious Anticipations

I am not saying this because I am in need, for I have
learned to be content whatever the circumstances.
PHILIPPIANS 4:11 NIV

Have you ever been so eager for the future that you forgot to be thankful for the present day?

Humans have a tendency to complain about the problems and irritations of life. It's much less natural to appreciate the good things we have—until they're gone. While it's fine to look forward to the future, let's remember to reflect on all of *today's* blessings—the large and the small—and appreciate all that we do have.

───────◦◦◦───────

Thank You, Lord, for the beauty of today. Please
remind me when I become preoccupied with the
future and forget to enjoy the present. Amen.

Walk Confidently

*"But blessed are those who trust in the LORD and have
made the LORD their hope and confidence."*
JEREMIAH 17:7 NLT

What gives you confidence? Is it your clothes. . .your money. . .your
skills? These are all good things, but they are blessings from God,
given to you through His grace. When your hopes (in other words,
your expectations for the future) rest only in God, then you can walk
confidently, knowing He will never disappoint you.

———————

*Lord, You are my hope and my confidence. I place all
my expectations for the future in You, knowing You will
never disappoint me. Thank You for Your love. Amen.*

Laugh a Rainbow

"When I see the rainbow in the clouds, I will remember the eternal covenant between God and every living creature on earth."

GENESIS 9:16 NLT

Ever feel like a cloud is hanging over your head? Sometimes the cloud darkens to the color of bruises, and we're deluged with cold rain that seems to have no end. When you're in the midst of one of life's thunderstorms, tape this saying to your mirror: Cry a river, laugh a rainbow. The rainbow, the symbol of hope God gave Noah after the flood, reminds us even today that every storm will eventually pass.

The rainbows You place in the sky after a storm are lovely reminders of the hope we have in You, God. Because of You, I know the storms of life are only temporary. . .and You will bring beauty from the storms.

Beautiful World

"Walk out into the fields and look at the wildflowers."
MATTHEW 6:28 MSG

Take the time to go outdoors. Look at nature. You don't have to spend hours to realize how beautiful God made the world. A single flower, if you really look at it, could be enough to fill you with awe. Sometimes we only need something very simple to remind us of God's grace.

———————

Creator, Father, I am amazed by Your creation and the goodness reflected in its beauty. Help me take time to enjoy this gift, to be filled to the brim with gratitude. Amen.

Simply Silly

A cheerful disposition is good for your health.
PROVERBS 17:22 MSG

Imagine the effect we could have on our world today if our countenance reflected the joy of the Lord all the time: at work, at home, at play. Jesus said, "I have told you this so that my joy may be in you and that your joy may be complete" (John 15:11 NIV). Is your cup of joy full? Have you laughed today? Not a small smile, but laughter. Maybe it's time we looked for something to laugh about and tasted joy. Jesus suggested it.

*Lord, help me find joy this day. Let me
laugh and give praises to the King. Amen.*

Grace for Each Day

May the Lord direct your hearts into
God's love and Christ's perseverance.
2 THESSALONIANS 3:5 NIV

Allow God to lead you each day. His grace will lead you deeper and deeper into the love of God—a love that heals your wounds and works through you to touch those around you. Just as Christ never gave up but let love lead Him all the way to the cross, so too God will direct you all the way, giving you the strength and the courage you need to face each challenge.

Lord, direct my heart into Your love and into
the perseverance of Christ. Lead me, by Your
grace, into a deeper love for You. Amen.

Release the Music Within

Those who are wise will find a time and a way to do what is right.
ECCLESIASTES 8:5 NLT

It has been said that many people go to their graves with their music still in them. Do you carry a song within your heart, waiting to be heard?

Whether we are eight or eighty, it is never too late to surrender our hopes and dreams to God. A wise woman trusts that God will help her find the time and manner in which to use her talents for His glory as she seeks His direction. Let the music begin.

———◆◆———

Dear Lord, my music is fading against the constant beat of a busy pace. I surrender my gifts to You and pray for the time and manner in which I can use those gifts to touch my world. Amen.

Shake It Up!

The LORD had said to Abram, "Leave your native country, your relatives, and your father's family, and go to the land that I will show you.... I will bless you...and you will be a blessing to others."
GENESIS 12:1–2 NLT

In God's wisdom, He likes to shake us up a little, stretch us out of our comfort zone, push us out on a limb. Yet we resist the change, cling to what's known and try to change His mind with fat, sloppy tears. Are you facing a big change? God wants us to be willing to embrace change He brings into our lives. Even unbidden change. You may feel as if you're out on a limb, but don't forget that God is the tree trunk. He's not going to let you fall.

———————

Holy, loving Father, in every area of my life,
teach me to trust You more deeply. Amen.

Marvelous Thunder

"God's voice thunders in marvelous ways; he does great things beyond our understanding."

JOB 37:5 NIV

Have you ever reflected deeply on the power that God is? Not that He *has*, but that He is.

Consider this: The One who controls nature also holds every one of our tears in His hand. He is our Father, and He works on our behalf. He is more than enough to meet our needs; He does things far beyond what our human minds can understand. This One who is power loves you. He looks at you and says, *"I delight in you, My daughter."* Wow! His ways are marvelous and beyond understanding.

———◆———

Lord God, You are power. You hold all things in Your hand and You chose to love me. You see my actions, hear my thoughts, watch my heartbreak. . .and You still love me. Please help me trust in Your power, never my own. Amen.

Masterpiece

*You made all the delicate, inner parts of my body
and knit me together in my mother's womb.*
PSALM 139:13 NLT

At the moment of your conception, roughly three million decisions were made about you. Everything from your eye color and the number of your wisdom teeth to the shape of your nose and the swirl of your fingerprints was determined in the blink of an eye. God is a big God. Unfathomable. Incomparable. Frankly, words just don't do Him justice. And He made *you*. You were knit together by a one-of-a-kind, amazing God who is absolutely, undeniably, head-over-heels crazy-in-love with you. Try to wrap your brain around that.

---

*Heavenly Father and Creator, thank You for the
amazing gift of life, for my uniqueness and individuality.
Help me use my life as a gift of praise to You. Amen.*

Power Up

The Spirit of God, who raised
Jesus from the dead, lives in you.
ROMANS 8:11 NLT

God is the same yesterday, today, and forever. His strength does not diminish over time. That same mountain-moving power you read about in the lives of people from the Old and New Testaments still exists today. We don't have to go it alone. Our heavenly Father wants to help. All we have to do is ask. He has already made His power available to His children. Whatever we face, wherever we go, whatever dreams we have for our lives, take courage and know that anything is possible when we draw on the power of God.

Father, help me remember that You are always
with me, ready to help me do all things. Amen.

Into God's Presence

"That person can pray to God and find favor with him, they will see God's face and shout for joy."

JOB 33:26 NIV

Prayer is the channel through which God's grace flows. We do not pray because God needs us to pray; we pray because we need to pray. When we come into God's presence, we are renewed. Our hearts lift. We look into the face of the One who loves us most, and we are filled with joy.

Father, thank You for the gift of prayer and the promise that I can talk with You at any time. As I look to You, fill my heart with Your joy. Amen.

Reach Out to Others

Whoever has the gift of encouraging others should encourage.
ROMANS 12:8 NCV

Just as God encourages us, He wants us to encourage others. The word *encourage* comes from Latin words that mean "to put heart or inner strength into someone." When God encourages us, His own heart reaches out to us and His strength becomes ours. As we rely on His grace, we are empowered to turn and reach out to those around us, lending them our hearts and strength.

———◆◆◆———

Lord, thank You for reaching out to me with Your heart and giving me Your strength. I pray that I would use that strength to encourage others. Amen.

How about Some Fun?

A twinkle in the eye means joy in the heart,
and good news makes you feel fit as a fiddle.
PROVERBS 15:30 MSG

God does not want His kids to be worn out and stressed out. A little relaxation, recreation—and, yes—*fun* are essential components of a balanced life. Even Jesus and His disciples found it necessary to get away from the crowds and pressures of ministry to rest. There's a lot of fun to be had out there—playing tennis or golf, jogging, swimming, painting, knitting, playing a musical instrument, visiting an art gallery, playing a board game, or going to a movie, a play, or a football game. Have you had any fun this week?

———————◦•◦———————

Lord, You are the One who gives balance to
my life. Help me to find time today for a little
relaxation, recreation, and even fun. Amen.

God's Mountain Sanctuary

*And seeing the multitudes, he went up into a
mountain. . .and. . .his disciples came unto him:
and he opened his mouth, and taught them.*
MATTHEW 5:1–2 KJV

Jesus often retreated to a mountain to pray. There He called His disciples to depart from the multitudes so that He could teach them valuable truths—the lessons we learn from nature. Do you yearn for a place where problems evaporate like the morning dew? Do you need a place of solace? God is wherever you are—behind a bedroom door, nestled alongside you in your favorite chair, or even standing at a sink full of dirty dishes. Come apart and enter God's mountain sanctuary.

———————

*Heavenly Father, I long to hear Your voice and to
flow in the path You clear before me. Help me find
sanctuary in Your abiding presence. Amen.*

Breathing

In certain ways we are weak, but the Spirit is here to help us. For example, when we don't know what to pray for, the Spirit prays for us in ways that cannot be put into words.

ROMANS 8:26 CEV

The Holy Spirit is the wind that blows through our world, breathing grace and life into everything that exists. He will breathe through you as well as you open yourself to Him. We need not worry about our own weakness or mistakes, for the Spirit will make up for them. His creative power will pray through us, work through us, and love through us.

Holy Spirit, thank You for interceding on my behalf, for breathing grace and life into me. Even through my weakness, thank You for Your power that carries my very breath to God. Amen.

Ladies in Waiting

I will wait for the LORD. . . I will put my trust in him.
ISAIAH 8:17 NIV

Do we want joy without accepting heartache? Peace without living through the stress? Patience without facing demands? God sees things differently. He's giving us the opportunity to learn through these delays, irritations, and struggles. Like Isaiah, we need to learn the art of waiting on God. He will come through every time—but in *His* time, not ours. The wait may be hours or days, or it could be years. But God is always faithful to provide for us. It is when we learn to wait on Him that we will find joy, peace, and patience through the struggle.

Father, You know what I need, so I will wait. Help me be patient, knowing You control my situation and that all good things come in Your time. Amen.

The Dream Maker

"What no eye has seen, what no ear has heard,
and what no human mind has conceived"—the
things God has prepared for those who love him.

1 CORINTHIANS 2:9 NIV

Dreams, goals, and expectations are part of our daily lives. We have an idea of what we want and how we're going to achieve it. Disappointment can raise its ugly head when what we wanted—what we expected—doesn't happen like we thought it should or doesn't happen as fast as we planned. God knows the dreams He has placed inside of you. He created you and knows what you can do—even better than you know yourself. Maintain your focus—not on the dream but on the Dream Maker—and together you will achieve your dream.

God, thank You for putting dreams in my heart. I refuse to quit.
I'm looking to You to show me how to reach my dreams. Amen.

People Pleaser vs. God Pleaser

We are not trying to please people but God, who tests our hearts.
1 THESSALONIANS 2:4 NIV

When we allow ourselves to be real before God, it doesn't matter what others think. If the God of the universe has accepted us, then who cares about someone else's opinion? It is impossible to please both God and man. We must make a choice. Man looks at the outward appearance, but God looks at the heart. Align your heart with His. Let go of impression management that focuses on outward appearance. Receive God's unconditional love and enjoy the freedom to be yourself before Him!

———— •◦• ————

Dear Lord, may I live for You alone. Help me transition from a people pleaser to a God pleaser. Amen.

When I Think of the Heavens

When I consider your heavens, the work of your fingers, the moon and the stars, which you have set in place, what is mankind that you are mindful of them, human beings that you care for them?
PSALM 8:3-4 NIV

Daughter of God, you are important to your heavenly Father, more important than the sun, the moon, and the stars. You are created in the image of God, and He cares for you. In fact, He cares so much that He sent His Son, Jesus, to offer His life as a sacrifice for your sins. The next time you look up at the heavens, the next time you ooh and aah over a majestic mountain or emerald waves crashing against the shoreline, remember that those things, in all their splendor, don't even come close to you—God's greatest creation.

———————⊷•⊶———————

O Father, when I look at everything You have created, I'm so overwhelmed with who You are. Who am I that You would think twice about me? And yet You do. You love me, and for that I'm eternally grateful! Amen.

Difficult People

*Do not turn your freedom into an opportunity for
the flesh, but through love serve one another.*
GALATIANS 5:13 NASB

Sometimes, like David, we need to turn our skirmishes with others over to the Lord. Then, by using our weapons—God's Word and a steadfast faith—we need to love and forgive others as God loves and forgives us. Although we may not like to admit it, we have all said and done some pretty awful things ourselves, making the lives of others difficult. Yet God has forgiven us *and* continues to love us. So do the right thing. Pull your feet out of the mire of unforgiveness, sidestep verbal retaliation, and stand tall in the freedom of love and forgiveness.

*The words and deeds of others have left me wounded and
bleeding. Forgiveness and love seem to be the last thing
on my mind. Change my heart, Lord. Help me to love and
forgive others as You love and forgive me. Amen.*

Unchained!

The Spirit you received does not make you slaves, so that you live in fear again; rather, the Spirit you received brought about your adoption to sonship. And by him we cry, "Abba, Father."

ROMANS 8:15 NIV

Do you struggle with fear? Do you feel it binding you with its invisible chains? If so, then there's good news. Through Jesus, you have received the Spirit of sonship. A son (or daughter) of the Most High God has nothing to fear. Knowing you've been set free is enough to make you cry, "Abba, Father!" in praise. Today, acknowledge your fears to the Lord. He will loose your chains and set you free.

Lord, thank You that You are the great chain breaker! I don't have to live in fear. I am Your child, Your daughter, and You are my Daddy-God! Amen.

Web of Love

*So now I am giving you a new commandment: Love each
other. Just as I have loved you, you should love each other.*
JOHN 13:34 NLT

God's grace comes to us through a net of relationships and connections. Because we know we are totally and unconditionally loved, we can in turn love others. The connections between us grow ever wider and stronger, a web of love that unites us all with God.

———————

*Jesus, I am grateful for the relationships You have
given me. Thank You for Your love that enables
me to love and be loved by others. Amen.*

Fix Your Thoughts on Truth

And now, dear brothers and sisters, one final thing.
Fix your thoughts on what is true, and honorable, and
right, and pure, and lovely, and admirable. Think about
things that are excellent and worthy of praise.

PHILIPPIANS 4:8 NLT

Dig through the Scriptures and find truths from God's Word to combat any false message that you may be struggling with. Write them down and memorize them. Here are a few to get started:

God looks at my heart, not my outward appearance. (1 Samuel 16:7)

I am free in Christ. (1 Corinthians 1:30)

I am a new creation. My old self is gone! (2 Corinthians 5:17)

The next time you feel negativity and false messages slip into your thinking, fix your thoughts on what you know to be true. Pray for the Lord to replace the doubts and negativity with His words of truth.

Lord God, please control my thoughts and help me
set my mind and heart on You alone. Amen.

Fill 'Er Up

"What strength do I have, that I should still hope?"
JOB 6:11 NIV

Run, rush, hurry, dash: a typical American woman's day. It's easy to identify with David's lament in Psalm 22:14 (NASB): "I am poured out like water. . .my heart is like wax; it is melted within me." Translation: I'm pooped; I'm numb; I'm drained dry. When we are at the end of our strength, God doesn't want us to lose hope of the refilling He can provide if we only lift our empty cups to Him.

---

*Fill me up, Lord! I need Your heavenly presence. . .
Your strength. . .Your comfort. Thank You for the
hope You provide in the daily-ness of life!*

Keep Breathing, Sister!

*As long as we are alive, we still have hope, just
as a live dog is better off than a dead lion.*
ECCLESIASTES 9:4 CEV

Isn't this a tremendous scripture? At first glance, the ending elicits a chuckle. But consider the truth it contains: Regardless of how powerful, regal, or intimidating a lion is, when he's dead, he's dead. But the living—you and I—still have hope. Limitless possibilities! Hope for today and for the future. Although we may be as lowly dogs, fresh, juicy bones abound. As long as we're breathing, it's not too late!

---

*God of possibilities, remind me it's never too late as
long as I'm breathing. Because of You, I have hope!*

The Ultimate Act of Love

Bring joy to your servant, Lord, for I put my trust in you. You, Lord, are forgiving and good, abounding in love to all who call to you.

PSALM 86:4–5 NIV

Forgiveness doesn't require that the person who did the hurting apologize or acknowledge what they've done. It's not about making the score even. It doesn't even require forgetting about the incident. But it is about admitting that the one who hurt us is human, just as we are. We surrender our right for revenge and, like God, let go and give the wrongdoer mercy, therefore blessing them.

———————

Gracious and loving Father, thank You that You love me and have forgiven me of my sins. May I be more like You in forgiving others. Although I may not be able to forgive as easily as You do, please encourage me to take those small steps. In forgiving others, Father, I am that much closer to being like You. Amen.

Grace Multiplied

*Honor the LORD with your wealth and with
the best part of everything you produce.*
PROVERBS 3:9 NLT

We connect the word *wealth* with money, but long ago the word meant "happiness, prosperity, well-being." If you think about your wealth in this light, then the word encompasses far more of your life. Your health, your abilities, your friends, your family, your physical strength, and your creative energy—all of these are parts of your true wealth. Grace brought all of these riches into your life, and when we use them to honor God, grace is multiplied still more.

———————

*Father, when I consider all the good things You
have given me, I am rich beyond belief. Help me
to graciously honor You with my wealth. Amen.*

Letting Go

A peaceful heart leads to a healthy body;
jealousy is like cancer in the bones.
PROVERBS 14:30 NLT

Some emotions are meant to be nourished, and others need to be quickly dropped into God's hands. Learn to cultivate and seek out that which brings peace to your heart. And practice letting go of your negative feelings as quickly as you can, releasing them to God. If you cling to these dark feelings, they will reproduce like a cancer, blocking the healthy flow of grace into your life.

———————

O God, search me and know my heart. Expose any
negative feelings in me. Help me leave them at the cross.
Cleanse me and fill my heart with Your peace. Amen.

Heaven's Perspective

Always give yourselves fully to the work of the Lord, because
you know that your labor in the Lord is not in vain.

1 CORINTHIANS 15:58 NIV

You may feel sometimes as though all of your hard work comes to nothing. But if your work is the Lord's work, you can trust Him to bring it to fulfillment. You may not always know what is being accomplished in the light of eternity, but God knows. And when you look back from heaven's perspective, you will be able to see how much grace was accomplished through all of your hard work.

God, when I don't see results, I sometimes get
discouraged in my work for You. Help me to remember
that You are busy doing things I cannot see. Amen.

A Continual Feast

The cheerful heart has a continual feast.
PROVERBS 15:15 NIV

Our choice of companions has much to do with our outlook. Negativity and positivity are both contagious. The writer of Proverbs says that a cheerful heart has a continual feast. So it's safe to assume that a grumpy heart will feel hungry and lacking, instead of full. While God calls us to minister to those who are hurting, we can do so with discernment. Next time someone complains, ask them to pray with you about their concerns. Tell them a story of how you overcame negativity or repaired a relationship. You might help turn their day around!

God, help me be a positive influence on my friends and family. Give me wisdom and the unwavering hope that comes from Christ, that I may share Your joy with others. Amen.

Why Praise God?

Though he slay me, yet will I trust in him.
JOB 13:15 KJV

It's difficult to praise God when problems press in harder than a crowd exiting a burning building. But that's the time to praise Him the most. We wait for our circumstances to change, while God desires to change us despite them. Praise coupled with prayer in our darkest moments is what moves the mighty hand of God to work in our hearts and lives. How can we pray and praise God when everything goes wrong? The bigger question might be: How can we not?

*Jesus, help me to pray and praise You
despite my circumstances. Amen.*

Look Up!

Your love, LORD, reaches to the heavens,
your faithfulness to the skies.
PSALM 36:5 NIV

In Bible times, people often studied the sky. Looking up at the heavens reminded them of God and His mighty wonders. A rainbow was God's sign to Noah that a flood would never again destroy the earth. God used a myriad of stars to foretell Abraham's abundant family, and a single star heralded Christ's birth. This immense space we call "sky" is a reflection of God's infinite love and faithfulness. So take time today. Look up at the heavens and thank God for His endless love.

Heavenly Father, remind me to stop and
appreciate Your wonderful creations. And as I
look upward, fill me with Your infinite love. Amen.

Thou Shalt Not Worry!

"Do not worry about tomorrow, for tomorrow will worry about itself. Each day has enough trouble of its own."
MATTHEW 6:34 NIV

What if the Lord had written an eleventh commandment: "Thou shalt not worry." In a sense, He did! He commands us in various scriptures not to fret. So cast your anxieties on the Lord. Give them up! Let them go! Don't let worries sap your strength and your joy. Today is a gift from the Lord. Don't sacrifice it to fears and frustrations! Let them go. . .and watch God work!

———————

Father God, lift all anxiety from my heart and make my spirit light again. I know I can't do it on my own. But with You I can let go. . .and watch You work! I praise You, God! Amen.

Never Failing. . .

My friends scorn me, but I pour out my tears to God.

JOB 16:20 NLT

Sometimes even the best of friends can let you down. Human beings aren't perfect. But God's grace will never fail you. When even your closest friends don't understand you, take your hurt to Him.

———◦◦———

Lord, when I feel alone and rejected, I am so grateful I can pour out my tears to You. Thank You for Your grace that never fails me. Amen.

The End of Your Rope

*Do not be far from me, for trouble is
near and there is no one to help.*

PSALM 22:11 NIV

Jesus reaches down and wraps you in His loving arms when you call to Him for help. The Bible tells us He is close to the brokenhearted (Psalm 34:18). We may not have the answers we are looking for here in this life, but we can be sure of this: God sees your pain and loves you desperately. Call to Him in times of trouble. If you feel that you're at the end of your rope, look up! His mighty hand is reaching toward you.

*Heavenly Father, I feel alone and afraid. Surround me
with Your love and give me peace and joy. Amen.*

The Details

*She is clothed with strength and dignity,
and she laughs without fear of the future.*
PROVERBS 31:25 NLT

God wants to clothe us with His strength and His dignity. He wants us to be whole and competent, full of His grace. When we are, we can look at the future and laugh, knowing God will take care of the details as we trust Him to be the foundation of our lives.

———◦◦◦———

Father, thank You for clothing me with strength and dignity. Thank You that I can look to my future without fear, confident You have all the details in Your hands. Amen.

Love Your Enemies

"Love your enemies, do good to them, and lend to them without expecting to get anything back. Then your reward will be great."
LUKE 6:35 NIV

God calls us to a love so brave, so intense that it defies logic and turns the world on its side. He calls us to love like He loves.

That means we must show patience where others have been short. We must show kindness where others have been cruel. We must look for ways to bless when others have cursed. God promises great rewards for those who do this. Oh, the rewards may not be immediate. But when God promises great rewards we can know without doubt that any present struggle will be repaid with goodness and blessing, many times over.

———————

Dear Father, help me to love those who hate me, bless those who curse me, and show kindness to those who have been cruel. Help me to love as You love. Amen.

Seasons of Change

The Spirit of God, who raised Jesus from the dead, lives in you.
And just as God raised Christ Jesus from the dead, he will give
life to your mortal bodies by this same Spirit living within you.

ROMANS 8:11 NLT

Change can be exciting or fearsome. Changing a habit or moving beyond your comfort zone can leave you feeling out of control. The power of God that formed the world, brought the dry land above the waters of the sea and raised Jesus from the dead is alive and active today. Imagine what it takes to overcome the natural laws of gravity to put the earth and seas in place. Imagine the power to bring the dead to life again. That same power is available to work out the details of your life.

———————

Lord, I want to grow and fulfill all You've destined me to be.
Help me to accept change and depend on Your strength
to make the changes I need in my life today. Amen.

Loving Sisters

But Ruth replied, "Don't urge me to leave you or to turn back from you. Where you go I will go, and where you stay I will stay. Your people will be my people and your God my God."

RUTH 1:16 NIV

The story of Ruth and Naomi is inspiring on many levels. Both women realized their commitment, friendship, and love for each other surpassed any of their differences. They were a blessing to each other. Do you have girlfriends who would do almost anything for you? A true friendship is a gift from God. Those relationships provide us with love, companionship, encouragement, loyalty, honesty, understanding, and more! Lasting friendships are essential to living a balanced life.

———— ⚬ ————

Father God, thank You for giving us the gift of friendship. May I be the blessing to my girlfriends that they are to me. Please help me to always encourage and love them and be a loving support for them in both their trials and their happiness. I praise You for my loving sisters! Amen.

O the Deep, Deep Love of Jesus

I pray that out of his glorious riches he may strengthen you with power through his Spirit in your inner being, so that Christ may dwell in your hearts through faith. And I pray that you, being rooted and established in love, may have power, together with all the Lord's holy people, to grasp how wide and long and high and deep is the love of Christ.

EPHESIANS 3:16–18 NIV

What an amazing picture. That He should care for us in such a way is almost incomprehensible. Despite our shortcomings, our sin, He loves us. It takes a measure of faith to believe in His love. When we feel a nagging thought of unworthiness, of being unlovable, trust in the Word and sing a new song. For His love is deep and wide.

Lord, thank You for loving me, even when I'm unlovable. Amen.

Focus Point

Therefore. . .stand firm. Let nothing move you.
1 CORINTHIANS 15:58 NIV

Some days stress comes at us from all directions. Our emotions are overwhelming. Life makes us dizzy. On days like that, don't worry about getting a lot accomplished—and don't try to make enormous leaps in your spiritual life. Instead, simply stand in one place. Like a ballet dancer who looks at one point to keep her balance while she twirls, fix your eyes on Jesus.

Jesus, when I get caught up in the whirlwind of stress and busyness and my own agenda, I can easily lose my balance. Help me fix my eyes on You. Amen.

Joyful in Glory

Let the saints be joyful in glory:
let them sing aloud upon their beds.
PSALM 149:5 KJV

When do you like to spend time alone with the Lord? In the morning, as the stillness of the day sweeps over you? At night, when you rest your head upon the pillow? Start your conversation with praise. Let your favorite worship song or hymn pour forth! Tell Him how blessed you are to be His child. This private praise time will strengthen you and will fill your heart with joy!

As I enter into this conversation with You, Father, I praise You.
Thank You for being Lord—and leader—of my life. Amen.

Joy in the Battle

*Then they returned, every man of Judah and Jerusalem, and
Jehoshaphat in the forefront of them, to go again to Jerusalem
with joy; for the LORD had made them to rejoice over their enemies.*

2 CHRONICLES 20:27 KJV

Enemy forces were just around the bend. Jehoshaphat, king of
Judah, called his people together. After much prayer, he sent the
worshippers (the Levites) to the front lines, singing joyful praises
as they went. The battle was won! When you face your next battle,
praise your way through it! Strength and joy will rise up within you!
Prepare for victory!

*No matter what kind of hardship I face, Father God,
I want to praise my way through it and come through
even stronger than I was before. Thank You for
helping me win life's battles, both large and small. Amen.*

Grace in Return

"Then those 'sheep' are going to say, 'Master, what are you talking about? When did we ever see you hungry and feed you, thirsty and give you a drink?...' Then the King will say, 'I'm telling the solemn truth: Whenever you did one of these things to someone overlooked or ignored, that was me—you did it to me.'"

MATTHEW 25:37-40 MSG

If Christ were sitting on our doorstep, lonely and tired and hungry, what would we do? We like to think we would throw the door wide open and welcome Him into our home. But the truth is we're given the opportunity to offer our hospitality to Jesus each time we're faced with a person in need. His grace reaches out to us through those who feel misunderstood and overlooked, and He wants us to offer that same grace back in return.

Jesus, open my eyes to the hungry and thirsty people all around me. Whether their hunger is spiritual or physical or both—help me to give them Your grace. Amen.

Mercy Multiplied

Mercy unto you, and peace, and love, be multiplied.
JUDE 2 KJV

Have you ever done the math on God's mercy? If so, you've probably figured out it just keeps multiplying itself out, over and over again. We mess up; He extends mercy. We mess up again; He pours out mercy once again. In the same way, peace, love, and joy are multiplied back to us. Praise the Lord! God's mathematics work in our favor.

———•◦•———

Father God, I am so thankful Your math
works differently from mine! Amen.

All of You

*"Love the Lord God with all your passion
and prayer and intelligence and energy."*
MARK 12:30 MSG

God wants all of you. He wants the "spiritual parts," but He also wants your emotions, your physical energy, and your brain's intelligence. Offer them all to God as expressions of your love for Him. Let His grace use every part of you!

―――――◆◆――――――

God, I sometimes forget You want all of me. I dedicate my emotions, my energy, and my intelligence to You. Enable me to offer these as expressions of Your love. Amen.

Longing for Home

This is what the LORD says: "You will be in Babylon for seventy years. But then I will come and do for you all the good things I have promised, and I will bring you home again."
JEREMIAH 29:10 NLT

Sometimes in life we go through periods when we feel out of place, as though we just don't belong. Our hearts feel restless and lonely. We long to go home, but we don't know how. God uses those times to teach us special things we need to know. But He never leaves us in exile. His grace always brings us home.

———◦•◦———

Father, when I am in a season of loneliness and restlessness, help me trust You to lead me home. Thank You for Your grace that guides me. Amen.

Linking Hearts with God

*"You will receive power when the Holy Spirit comes on you;
and you will be my witnesses. . .to the ends of the earth."*
ACTS 1:8 NIV

God knows our hearts. He knows what we need to make it through
a day. So in His kindness, He gave us a gift in the form of the Holy
Spirit. As a Counselor, a Comforter, and a Friend, the Holy Spirit
acts as our inner compass. He upholds us when times are hard and
helps us hear God's directions. When the path of obedience grows
dark, the Spirit floods it with light. What revelation! He lives within
us. Therefore, our prayers are lifted to the Father, to the very throne
of God!

*Father God, how blessed I am to come into Your presence.
Help me, Father, when I am weak. Guide me this day. Amen.*

Thankful, Thankful Heart

I will praise you, LORD, with all my heart.
I will tell all the miracles you have done.
PSALM 9:1 NCV

When you choose to approach life from the positive side, you can find thankfulness in most of life's circumstances. It completely changes your outlook, your attitude, and your countenance. When you are tempted to feel sorry for yourself or to blame others or God for difficulties, push PAUSE. Take a moment and rewind your life. Look back and count the blessings God has given you. As you remind yourself of all He has done for you and in you, it will bring change to your attitude and give you hope in the situation you're facing. Count your blessings today.

Lord, I am thankful for my life and all You have done
for me. When life happens, help me to respond to it in a
healthy, positive way. Remind me to look to You and trust
You to carry me through life's challenges. Amen.

Transformed

And Sarah declared, "God has brought me laughter.
All who hear about this will laugh with me."
GENESIS 21:6 NLT

The first time we read of Sarah laughing, it was because she doubted God. She didn't believe that at her age she would have a baby. But God didn't hold her laughter against her. Instead, He transformed it. He turned her laughter of scorn and doubt into the laughter of fulfillment and grace.

Father Redeemer, thank You for taking my very worst
moments and transforming them into a story You can
use for Your purpose and Your glory. Amen.

He Carries Us

In his love and mercy he redeemed them. He lifted them up and carried them through all the years.
ISAIAH 63:9 NLT

Are you feeling broken today? Depressed? Defeated? Run to Jesus and not away from Him.

He will carry us—no matter what pain we have to endure. No matter what happens to us. God sent Jesus to be our Redeemer. He knew the world would hate, malign, and kill Jesus. Yet He allowed His very flesh to writhe in agony on the cross—so we could also become His sons and daughters. He loves me, and you, that much.

———————

Lord Jesus, thank You for coming to us—for not abandoning us when we are broken. Thank You for Your work on the cross, for Your grace, mercy, and love. Help me to seek You even when I can't feel You, to love You even when I don't know all the answers. Amen.

Standing Firm

*I. . .didn't dodge their insults, faced them as they spit
in my face. And the Master, GOD, stays right there
and helps me, so I'm not disgraced. Therefore I set my
face like flint, confident that I'll never regret this. My
champion is right here. Let's take our stand together!*

ISAIAH 50:6-8 MSG

Isaiah reminds us that we are not alone in our battles—even when
everyone is against us and we feel outnumbered and outmaneu-
vered. But remember, your champion, God, is right there, saying, *"I
am not leaving you! We are sticking this out together. You can put
your chin up confidently, knowing that I, the Sustainer, am on your
side. Let's take our stand together!"*

*Lord, boldly stand beside me. May the strength of
Your arms gird me as I take a stand for You. Lift my
chin today; give me confidence to face opposition,
knowing You are right there with me. Amen.*

Encourage One Another

*Therefore encourage one another and build each
other up, just as in fact you are doing.*
1 THESSALONIANS 5:11 NIV

Encouragement is more than words. It is also valuing, being tolerant of, serving, and praying for one another. It is looking for what is good and strong in a person and celebrating it. Encouragement means sincerely forgiving and asking for forgiveness, recognizing someone's weaknesses and holding out a helping hand, giving humbly while building someone up, helping others to hope in the Lord, and praying God will encourage them in ways you cannot. Whom will you encourage today? Get in the habit of encouraging others. It will bless them and you.

*Heavenly Father, open my eyes to those who need
encouragement. Show me how I can help. Amen.*

Open to Joy

"The joy of the LORD is your strength."
NEHEMIAH 8:10 NIV

Our God is a God of joy. He is not a God of sighing and gloom. Open yourself to His joy. It is a gift of grace He longs to give you. He knows it will make you strong.

———◆◆◆———

O Lord, Giver of joy and Source of my strength, thank
You for these gifts, which are mine in abundance.
Help me rely on Your joy and strength. Amen.

Magnifying Life

My soul will make its boast in the LORD; the humble
will hear it and rejoice. O magnify the LORD with
me, and let us exalt His name together.
PSALM 34:2-3 NASB

Mary knew she was the object of God's favor and mercy. That knowledge produced humility. Try as we might, we can't produce this humility in ourselves. It is our natural tendency to be self-promoters . . .to better our own reputations. We need the help of the Spirit to remind us that God has favored each of us with His presence. He did not have to come to us in Christ, but He did. He has chosen to set His love on us. His life redeemed ours, and He sanctifies us. We are recipients of the action of His grace.

Christ Jesus, help me remember what You have done for
me and desire for others to see and know You. Amen.

Pray about Everything

The LORD directs the steps of the godly.
He delights in every detail of their lives.
PSALM 37:23 NLT

The Bible says that the Lord delights in every detail of His children's lives. And no matter how old a believer is, they are and always will be God's child.

Adult prayers don't have to be well ordered and formal. God loves hearing His children's voices, and no detail is too little or dull to pray about. Tell God you hope the coffee house will have your favorite pumpkin-spice latte on their menu. Ask Him to give you patience as you wait in line. Thank Him for how wonderful that coffee tastes! Get into the habit of talking with Him all day long, because He loves you and delights in all facets of your life.

Dear God, teach me to pray about everything
with childlike innocence and faith. Amen.

Trust Him

You people who are now crying are blessed,
because you will laugh with joy.
LUKE 6:21 NCV

God's grace comes to you even in the midst of tears. He is there with you in your hurt and your sadness. Trust in Him, knowing sadness does not last forever. One day you will laugh again.

———————

Father, even in my darkest days, bestow on me Your
grace. Thank You for the promise that my tears will not
last and that You will replace them with joy. Amen.

He's Waiting. . .

"The eyes of the LORD watch over those who do right, and his ears are open to their prayers."
1 PETER 3:12 NLT

You don't have to try to get God's attention. He is watching you right now. His ear is tuned to your voice. All you need to do is speak, and He will hear you. Receive the gift of grace He gives to you through prayer. Tell God your thoughts, your feelings, your hopes, your joys. He's waiting to listen to you.

Father, what a comfort it is to know You are watching over me and that Your ears are always open to my prayers. Thank You for the gift of Your presence. Amen.

Near at Hand

Quiet down before GOD, be prayerful before him.

PSALM 37:7 MSG

It's not easy to be quiet. Our world is loud, and the noise seeps into our hearts and minds. We feel restless and jumpy, on edge. God seems far away. But God is always near at hand, no matter how we feel. When we quiet our hearts, we will find Him there, patiently waiting, ready to show us His grace.

Lord, when my heart is restless and jumpy, remind me
You are near, waiting to comfort me with Your love. Quiet
me with Your nearness. Show me Your grace. Amen.

Is Anyone Listening?

"And I will ask the Father, and He will give you another Helper (Comforter, Advocate, Intercessor—Counselor, Strengthener, Standby), to be with you forever."

JOHN 14:16 AMP

Our heavenly Father wants to hear from us. He cares so much that He sent the Holy Spirit to be our Counselor, our Comforter. When we pray—when we tell God our needs and give Him praise—He listens. Then He directs the Spirit within us to speak to our hearts and give us reassurance. Our world is filled with noise and distractions. Look for a place where you can be undisturbed for a few minutes. Take a deep breath, lift your prayers, and listen. God will speak—and your heart will hear.

Dear Lord, I thank You for Your care. Help me recognize Your voice and listen well. Amen.

Beyond Intelligence

The fastest runner does not always win the race, the strongest soldier does not always win the battle, the wisest does not always have food, . . . Time and chance happen to everyone.

ECCLESIASTES 9:11 NCV

How smart do you think you are? Do you assume you will be able to think your way through life's problems? Many of us do—but God reminds us some things are beyond the scope of our intelligence. Some days life simply doesn't make sense. But even then, grace is there with us in the chaos. When we can find no rational answers to life's dilemmas, we have no choice but to rely absolutely on God.

———————

God, I am conditioned to rely on strength, speed, and efficiency. While those things are useful, I know wisdom is more important. Help me seek answers directly from You. Amen.

Another Moment Longer

Wait patiently for the LORD. Be brave and
courageous. Yes, wait patiently for the LORD.
PSALM 27:14 NLT

Patience is all about waiting things out. It's about holding on another moment longer. It means enduring hard times. As a younger person, you probably felt you couldn't possibly endure certain things; but the older you get, the more you realize you can. If you just wait long enough, the tide always turns. Hold on. Your life will change. God's grace will rescue you.

———————

Lord, help me wait patiently for You. Help me be
brave and courageous. Remind me the tide always
turns and You will come through for me. Amen.

One Thing Is Needed

"Martha, Martha," the Lord answered, "you are worried and upset about many things, but few things are needed—or indeed only one."
LUKE 10:41–42 NIV

We are each given twenty-four hours in a day. Einstein and Edison were given no more than Joseph and Jeremiah of the Old Testament. Since God has blessed each of us with twenty-four hours, let's seek His direction on how to spend this invaluable commodity wisely—giving more to people than things, spending more time on relationships than the rat race. In Luke, our Lord reminded dear, dogged, drained Martha that only one thing is needed—Him.

Father God, oftentimes I get caught up in the minutia of life. The piled laundry can appear more important than the people around me. Help me use my time wisely. Open my eyes to see what is truly important. Amen.

No More Sting

O death, where is thy sting? O grave, where is thy victory?
1 CORINTHIANS 15:55 KJV

We have a choice to make. We can either live life in fear or live life by faith. Fear and faith cannot coexist. Jesus Christ has conquered our greatest fear—death. He rose victorious and has given us eternal life through faith. Knowing this truth enables us to face our fears with courage. There is no fear that cannot be conquered by faith. Let's not panic but trust the Lord instead. Let's live by faith and experience the victory that has been given to us through Jesus Christ, our Lord.

Lord, You alone know my fears. Help me trust You more.
May I walk in the victory You have purchased for me. Amen.

Act in Love

Let all that you do be done in love.
1 CORINTHIANS 16:14 NASB

Because love is not merely an emotion, it needs to become real through action. We grow in love as we act in love. Some days the emotion may overwhelm us; other days we may feel nothing at all. But if we express our love while making meals, driving the car, talking to our families, or cleaning the house, God's love will flow through us to the world around us—and we will see His grace at work.

Father, when I feel love, it's easy to show it. But the feelings are not always there. Help me find ways to express Your love obediently through all my actions. Amen.

A Very Important Phrase

And it came to pass. . .

FOUND MORE THAN 400 TIMES IN THE KING JAMES BIBLE

There are times in life when we think we can't bear one more day, one more hour, one more minute. But no matter how bad things seem at the time, they are temporary. What's really important is how we handle the opportunities before us today, whether we let our trials defeat us or look for the hand of God in everything. Every day, week, and year are made up of things that "come to pass"—so even if we fail, we needn't be disheartened. Other opportunities—better days—will come. Let's look past those hard things today and glorify the name of the Lord.

Lord Jesus, how awesome it is that You send or allow these little things that will pass. May we recognize Your hand in them today and praise You for them. Amen.

No Matter What

*Be thankful in all circumstances, for this is God's
will for you who belong to Christ Jesus.*

1 THESSALONIANS 5:18 NLT

Jesus enables us to be thankful, and He is the cause of our thankfulness. *No matter what happens,* we know Jesus has given up His life to save ours. He has sacrificed Himself on the cross so we may live life to the fullest. And while "to the fullest" means we will experience pain as well as joy, we must *always* be thankful—regardless of our circumstances—for the love we experience in Christ Jesus.

*Dear Lord, thank You for Your love. Please let me
be thankful, even in the midst of hardships. You
have blessed me beyond measure. Amen.*

Listening Closely

I will listen to what God the LORD says.
PSALM 85:8 NIV

In today's hurried world, with all of the surrounding noise, it's easy to ignore the still, small voice nudging us in the right direction. We fire off requests, expect microwave-instant answers and get aggravated when nothing happens. Our human nature demands a response. How will we know what to do/think/say if we do not listen? As the worship song "Speak to My Heart" so beautifully puts it, when we are "yielded and still," then He can "speak to my heart."

Listening is a learned art, too often forgotten in the busyness of a day. The alarm clock buzzes: We hit the floor running, toss out a prayer, maybe sing a song of praise, grab our car keys and are out the door. If only we'd slow down and let the heavenly Father's words sink into our spirits, what a difference we might see in our prayer life. This day, stop. Listen. See what God has in store for you.

Lord, how I want to surrender and seek Thy will.
Please still my spirit and speak to me. Amen.

Grace of Hospitality

When God's people are in need, be ready to help them. Always be eager to practice hospitality.

ROMANS 12:13 NLT

God opens Himself to you, offering you everything He has, and He calls you to do the same for others. Just as He made you welcome, make others welcome in your life. Don't reach out to others grudgingly, with a sense of obligation. Instead, be eager for opportunities to practice the grace of hospitality.

Father, although I long to help others in need, I can sure find a lot of excuses to avoid practicing hospitality. Please give me an eagerness to share with others. Amen.

Christ Followers

*"This is what the L ord All-Powerful says: 'Do what is
right and true. Be kind and merciful to each other.'"*
ZECHARIAH 7:9 NCV

As Christ's followers, we need to interact with others the way He
did when He was on earth. That means we don't lie to each other,
and we don't use others. Instead, we practice kindness and mercy.
We let God's grace speak through our mouths.

*Lord All-Powerful, thank You for the blessing of relationships.
Help me to do what is right and true, to be kind and merciful to
others. Give me Your grace always. Speak through me. Amen.*

Sleep in Peace

*At day's end I'm ready for sound sleep, for you,
GOD, have put my life back together.*

PSALM 4:8 MSG

At the end of the day, let everything—good and bad together—drop into God's hands. You can sleep in peace, knowing that meanwhile God will continue to work, healing all that is broken in your life. Relax in His grace.

———————

Father, thank You for the gift of rest—a time to put the busyness aside. When I wake, things make much more sense. Thank You for putting my life back together! Amen.

Unchanged

*Why am I discouraged? Why is my heart
so sad? I will put my hope in God!*
PSALM 42:5 NLT

Thousands of years ago, the psalmist who wrote these words expressed the same feelings we all have. Some days we just feel blue. The world looks dark, everything seems to be going wrong, and our hearts are sad. Those feelings are part of the human condition. Like the psalmist, we need to remind ourselves that God is unchanged by cloudy skies and gloomy hearts. His grace is always the same, as bright and hopeful as ever.

*Heavenly Father, when I am overcome by sadness, help me see
Your light shimmering just beyond the clouds. Thank You for Your
grace, which is a bright promise and a great comfort. Amen.*

Strong in Christ

I can do all things through Christ who strengthens me.
PHILIPPIANS 4:13 NKJV

Left to ourselves, we are weak. We make mistakes. We fall short of our goals. But in Christ we are strong. By His grace we can accomplish anything.

*Jesus, I am conditioned to believe that weakness
is something to be despised. Help me to see
weakness differently—remembering that my
weakness is a conduit for Your strength. Amen.*

Joy in the Morning

All who seek the LORD will praise him.
Their hearts will rejoice with everlasting joy.
PSALM 22:26 NLT

Every day God provides us with beauty all around to cheer and help us. It may come through the beauty of flowers or the bright blue sky—or maybe the white snow covering the trees of a glorious winter wonderland. It may be through the smile of a child or the grateful face of the one we care for. Each and every day, the Lord has a special gift to remind us of whose we are and to generate the joy we need to succeed.

———————

Lord God, thank You for Your joy; thank You for providing
it every day to sustain me. I will be joyful in You. Amen.

Sharing Life

But if we walk in the light, God himself being the light,
we also experience a shared life with one another.
1 JOHN 1:7 MSG

Some of us are extroverts, and some of us are introverts. But either way, God asks us to share our lives in some way with others. As we walk in His light, He gives us grace to experience a new kind of life, a life we have in common with the others who share His kingdom.

———————

Lord Jesus, I recognize You have asked me to share
my life with others. Help me look for opportunities to
make connections as I walk in Your light. Amen.

Renewal

"Look, the winter is past, and the rains are over and gone."
SONG OF SOLOMON 2:11 NLT

Dreary times of cold and rain come to us all. Just as the earth needs those times to renew itself, so do we. As painful as those times are, grace works through them to make us into the people God has called us to be. But once those times are over, there's no need to continue to dwell on them. Go outside and enjoy the sunshine!

———◦•◦———

Father, it's easy to become discouraged during the long days of winter. But I know times of darkness are necessary to fully appreciate the joy of light. Help me to revel in Your sunlight. Amen.

Thrive!

Those who trust in their riches will fall,
but the righteous will thrive like a green leaf.
PROVERBS 11:28 NIV

Money seems so important in our world. Many things we want depend on money—that remodeling project we're hoping to do, the Christmas gifts we want to give, the vacation we hope to take, and the new car we want to drive. There's nothing wrong with any of those things, but our enjoyment of them will always be fleeting. Only God's daily grace makes us truly grow and thrive.

Father, remind me that while caring for my family, making money, and preparing for my future are good things, they are not my identity. Help me find my purpose, my worth, in You. Amen.

Back to God

My dear brothers and sisters, always be willing to listen and slow to speak. Do not become angry easily, because anger will not help you live the right kind of life God wants.

JAMES 1:19–20 NCV

Our feelings are gifts from God, and we should never be ashamed of them. Instead, we need to offer them all back to God, both our joys and our frustrations. When we give God our anger, our irritation, our hurt feelings, and our frustrations, we make room in our hearts to truly hear what others are saying.

Father, as uncomfortable as my feelings can be sometimes, thank You for what they teach me. Help me trust You with all my feelings so I can be a good listener. Amen.

Light in the Dark

The light shines in the darkness,
and the darkness has not overcome it.

JOHN 1:5 NIV

Jesus said in John 12:46 (NIV), "I have come into the world as a light, so that no one who believes in me should stay in darkness." He also promised He is always with us. Because we have Him we have light. If we fail to perceive it, if we seem to be living in darkness, perhaps we have turned our backs to the light of His countenance. Maybe we are covering our eyes with the cares of this world. Clouds of sin may be darkening our lives, but He has not left us. He promises us that in following Him we will not walk in darkness but have the light of life.

———————◆◆◆———————

Lord Jesus, show me my blind spots. Where am I
covering my own eyes or walking away from You?
Turn me back to You, the Light of life.

The Perfect Reflection

"Give careful thought to your ways."
HAGGAI 1:7 NIV

As we give careful thought to our ways, we should first look back to where we have come from and reflect on God's work in our lives. We are on a journey. Sometimes the road is difficult; sometimes the road is easy. We must consider where we were when God found us and where we are now through His grace. Even more important, we must think about the ways our present actions, habits, and attitude toward God reflect our lives as Christians. Only when we are able to honestly assess our lives in Christ can we call on His name to help perfect our reflection.

*Dear Lord, help me look honestly at the ways I live
and make changes where necessary. Amen.*

Amazing Love

Your unfailing love, O Lord, is as vast as the heavens;
your faithfulness reaches beyond the clouds.
PSALM 36:5 NLT

God loves you. The Creator of the universe cares about you, and His love is unconditional and limitless. You can never make Him tired of you; He will never abandon you. You are utterly and completely loved, no matter what, forever and ever. Isn't that amazing?

———————◆◆———————

O Father, I am so grateful for Your unfailing love, vast as the heavens, reaching beyond the clouds. Thank You for never abandoning me and for Your amazing grace. Amen.

Today and Tomorrow

*You are my strong shield, and I trust you completely. You have
helped me, and I will celebrate and thank you in song.*

PSALM 28:7 CEV

God proves Himself to us over and over again. And yet over and
over we doubt His power. We need to learn from experience. The
God whose strength rescued us yesterday and the day before will
certainly rescue us again today. As we celebrate the grace we received
yesterday and the day before, we gain confidence and faith for
today and tomorrow.

———————◆◆◆———————

*My Father, my Strong Shield, You have proved Yourself
to me over and over again. Remind me of Your goodness.
I praise You and celebrate Your faithfulness. Amen.*

Ever Wider

A longing fulfilled is a tree of life.
PROVERBS 13:12 NIV

Take stock of your life. What were you most hoping to achieve a year ago? (Or five years ago?) How many of those goals have been achieved? Sometimes, once we've reached a goal, we move on too quickly to the next one, never allowing ourselves to find the grace God wants to reveal within that achievement. With each goal reached, His grace spreads out into your life, like a tree whose branches grow ever wider.

God, help me to find the balance between moving forward and looking back. Give me moments to pause and reflect on how far I have come with Your grace. Amen.

Finish Line

*I have fought the good fight, I have
finished the race, I have kept the faith.*

2 TIMOTHY 4:7 NIV

Paul felt his life was coming to an end. As he wrote to his friend
Timothy, he spoke of this. He was not boasting; he was just giving his
status report, as it were. Good fight fought? Check. Race finished?
Check (well, almost). Faith kept? Check. What does your checklist
include? What accomplishments make your list? What goals do you
want to be known for achieving? What do you want to do, whom do
you want to become, before your race is finished? Write them down
today. Put a checkbox by each one. Then go and work out your life,
faith, and ministry for all you're worth. Godspeed.

---

*Dear Lord, bless the work of my hands and feet. Make
me Your servant so that at the end of my life I can look
forward to hearing You say, "Well done." Amen.*

Promises of God

"For the LORD your God is living among you. He is a mighty savior. He will take delight in you with gladness. With his love, he will calm all your fears. He will rejoice over you with joyful songs."
ZEPHANIAH 3:17 NLT

Look at all the promises packed into this one verse of Scripture! God is with you. He is your mighty savior. He delights in you with gladness. He calms your fears with His love. He rejoices over you with joyful songs. Wow! What a bundle of hope is found here for the believer. Like a mother attuned to her newborn baby's cries, so is your heavenly Father's heart for you. He delights in being your Father. You are blessed to be a daughter of the King.

*Father, thank You for loving me the way
You do. You are all I need. Amen.*

Law of Love

I pondered the direction of my life,
and I turned to follow your laws.

PSALM 119:59 NLT

Did you know that the word *law* comes from root words that mean "foundation" or "something firm and fixed"? Sometimes we can't help but feel confused and uncertain. When that happens, turn to God's law, His rule for living. Love is His law, the foundation that always holds firm. When we cling to that, we find direction.

Lord, when I ponder the direction of my life without Your Spirit, I am lost and uncertain. Thank You for Your Word that anchors me in truth and provides the guidance I need. Amen.

Light My Path

Your word is a lamp for my feet, a light on my path.
PSALM 119:105 NIV

God's Word is like a streetlamp. Often we *think* we know where we're going and where the stumbling blocks are. We believe we can avoid pitfalls and maneuver the path successfully on our own. But the truth is that without God's Word we are walking in darkness, stumbling and tripping. When we sincerely begin to search God's Word, we find the path becomes clear. God's light allows us to live our lives in the most fulfilling way possible, a way planned out from the very beginning by God Himself.

Jesus, shine Your light upon my path. I have spent too long wandering through the darkness, looking for my way. As I search Your Word, I ask You to make it a lamp to my feet so I can avoid the pitfalls of the world and walk safely along the path You have created specifically for me. Amen.

Thinking Habits

*And now, dear brothers and sisters, one final thing.
Fix your thoughts on what is true, and honorable, and
right, and pure, and lovely, and admirable. Think about
things that are excellent and worthy of praise.*

PHILIPPIANS 4:8 NLT

Our brains are gifts from God, intended to serve us well, special gifts of grace we often take for granted. In return, we need to offer our minds back to God. Practice thinking positive thoughts. Focus on what is true rather than on lies; pay attention to beautiful things and stop staring at the ugly things in life. Discipline your mind to take on God's habits of thinking.

---

*Heavenly Father, thank You for my brain, a gift from You. Help
me focus on things that honor You. Open my eyes to beautiful,
positive things—and, most important, to Your truth. Amen.*

Looking Forward

*I focus on this one thing: Forgetting the past
and looking forward to what lies ahead.*
PHILIPPIANS 3:13 NLT

As followers of Christ, we are people who look forward rather than backward. We have all made mistakes, but God does not want us to dwell on them, wallowing in guilt and discouragement. Instead, He calls us to let go of the past, trusting Him to deal with it. His grace is new every moment.

———◆◆———

*Father, I sometimes ruminate over past mistakes. Help me
not to wallow in the past—instead, enable me to delight
in Your grace, which is new each moment. Amen.*

Seeking God's Plan

*For we are His workmanship, created in Christ
Jesus for good works, which God prepared
beforehand that we should walk in them.*

EPHESIANS 2:10 NKJV

How can you know God's plans for your life? First, you should
meet with Him in prayer each day and seek His will. Studying the
Bible is also important. Often, God speaks to us directly through
His Word (Psalm 119:105). Finally, you must have faith that God *will*
work out His plan for your life and that His plan is good. Jeremiah
29:11 (NIV) says, "'For I know the plans I have for you,' declares the
LORD, 'plans to prosper you and not to harm you, plans to give you
hope and a future.'" Are you living in Christ's example and seeking
God's plan for your life?

*Father, what is Your plan for me? I know it is good.
Reveal it to me, Lord. Speak to me through prayer.*

Joyful, Patient and Faithful

Be joyful in hope, patient in affliction, faithful in prayer.
ROMANS 12:12 NIV

Faithfulness in prayer requires discipline. God is faithful regardless of our attitude toward Him. He never changes, wavers, or forsakes His own. We may be faithful to do daily tasks around the house. We feed the cat, wash the clothes, and empty the trash. But faithfulness in the quiet discipline of prayer is harder. There are seemingly no consequences for neglecting our time with the Lord. Oh, what a myth this is! Set aside a daily time for prayer and see how the Lord blesses you, transforming your spirit to increase your joyful hope, your patience, and your faithfulness.

Faithful God, find me faithful. Stir up the hope and joy within me. Give me the grace I need to wait on You. Amen.

Cherished Desire

God our Father loves us. He is kind and has given
us eternal comfort and a wonderful hope.
2 THESSALONIANS 2:16 CEV

Webster's definition of hope: "to cherish a desire with expectation." In other words, yearning for something wonderful you expect to occur. Our hope in Christ is not just yearning for something wonderful, as in "I hope for a sunny beach day." It's a deep trust with roots that extend from the beginning of time to the infinite future. Our hope is not just the anticipation of heaven, but the expectation of a fulfilling life walking beside our Creator and best Friend.

———————

Dear heavenly Father, I want to journey through life in hopeful
expectation—always anticipating You'll work in wonderful ways!

How Should I Talk to God?

"This, then, is how you should pray: 'Our Father in heaven, hallowed be your name, your kingdom come, your will be done, on earth as it is in heaven. Give us today our daily bread. And forgive us our debts, as we also have forgiven our debtors. And lead us not into temptation, but deliver us from the evil one.' "

MATTHEW 6:9-13 NIV

Jesus gave us an example of how to pray in His famous petition that was recorded in Matthew 6:9-13. We don't need to suffer with an anxious heart or feel ensnared by this world with no one to hear our cry for help. We can talk to God, right now, and He will listen. The act of prayer is as simple as launching a boat into the Sea of Galilee, but it's as miraculous as walking on water.

———————

God, how wonderful it is that You hear me when I call out to You and that You answer with exactly what I need. Amen.

Harm for Good

"You meant evil against me, but God meant it for good."
GENESIS 50:20 NASB

Joseph suffered more in his lifetime than any of us ever will. But God remembered him, blessed him, and made him a man of great authority in the land so that he was in the position to make wise decisions and save many people from starvation.

Instead of feeling entitled to apologies, Joseph wanted redemption in place of revenge. In response to his brothers' wanting security, he replied, "Don't be afraid. Am I in the place of God? You intended to harm me, but God intended it for good to accomplish what is now being done, the saving of many lives" (Genesis 50:19-20 NIV).

Maybe you're in the middle of suffering right now, so deep in it you can't possibly see any good. Take encouragement from Joseph's words. You are not God—you cannot see what He sees. Maybe yet there will be some good that comes out of the harm.

Dear God, help me to trust in Your plans. Amen.

Get Real

The Lord says: "These people come near to me with their mouth and honor me with their lips, but their hearts are far from me. Their worship of me is based on merely rules they have been taught."
ISAIAH 29:13 NIV

The world is full of hypocrites. To be honest, sometimes the church is too—hypocrites who profess to know and honor God, but when it comes right down to it, they are only going through the motions of religion. Their hearts are far from Him. Take the time to find out who God is, what He has done for you, and why He is worthy of your devotion. Following God is not about a bunch of man-made rules. He loves you; He sent His Son to die for you; and He longs to have a deep, personal relationship with you. Get real with God and get real with yourself!

Dear God, reveal Yourself to me. Show me who You are and show me how to live so that I honor You not only with my lips, but with my heart as well. Amen.

I Think I Can

"Do not be afraid; only believe."
MARK 5:36 NKJV

Take a trip through the Bible and you'll see that those God asked to do the impossible were ordinary people of their day; yet they demonstrated that they believed God saw something in them they didn't see. He took ordinary men and women and used them to do extraordinary things. When you believe you can do something, your faith goes to work. You rise to the challenge, which enables you to go further than before, to do more than you thought possible. Consider trying something new—if you think you can, you can!

God, I want to have high expectations. I want to do more than most think I can do. Help me to reach higher and do more as You lead me. Amen.

The Answer Is No One

The LORD is my light and my salvation—whom shall I fear?
PSALM 27:1 NIV

When you accept Christ as your Savior, you get certain things in return. You get an understanding of good and evil—and you get the knowledge that you are on the side of good. You get a clearer vision of the darkness in your life—and you get a Friend who is always with you, no matter how dark things seem to be. And you get peace—through knowing your place before God. That you stand in His grace, blameless and pure, and you have a place in heaven created just for you. A place no one can take away.

Dear Jesus, help me to feel You at my side. Amen.

God Cares for You

"Consider how the wild flowers grow. They do not labor or spin. Yet I tell you, not even Solomon in all his splendor was dressed like one of these. If that is how God clothes the grass of the field, which is here today, and tomorrow is thrown into the fire, how much more will he clothe you—O you of little faith!"

LUKE 12:27-28 NIV

If God makes the flowers, each type unique and beautiful, and if He sends the rain and sun to meet their needs, will He not care for you as well?

He made you. What the Father makes, He loves. And that which He loves, He cares for. We were made in His image. Humans are dearer to God than any of His other creations. Rest in Him. Trust Him. Just as He cares for the birds of the air and the flowers of the meadows, God is in the business of taking care of His sons and daughters. Let Him take care of you.

———◆◆◆———

Father, I am amazed by Your creation.
Remind me that I am Your treasured child.
Take care of me today as only You can do. Amen.

Be Still

*Thou wilt keep him in perfect peace, whose mind
is stayed on thee: because he trusteth in thee.*
ISAIAH 26:3 KJV

Longing for His children to know His peace, God sent prophets like Isaiah to stir up faith, repentance, and comfort in the hearts of the "chosen people."

God's message is just as applicable today as it was back then. By keeping our minds fixed on Him, we can have perfect, abiding peace even in the midst of a crazy world. The path to peace is not easy, but it is simple: Focus on God. As we meditate on His promises and His faithfulness, He gets bigger, while our problems get smaller.

*God, when I focus on the world, my mind and
heart feel anxious. Help me to keep my mind on
You, so that I can have hope and peace.*

He Has Chosen You

Therefore, as God's chosen people, holy and
dearly loved, clothe yourselves with compassion,
kindness, humility, gentleness and patience.
COLOSSIANS 3:12 NIV

No matter how athletic, beautiful, popular, or smart you are, you've probably experienced a time when you were chosen last or overlooked entirely. Being left out is a big disappointment of life on earth.

The good news is that this disappointment isn't part of God's kingdom. Even when others forget about us, God doesn't. He has handpicked His beloved children now and forever. The truth is that Jesus died for *everyone*—every man, woman, and child who has ever lived and will ever live. The Father chooses us all. All we have to do is grab a glove and join the team.

Father, thanks for choosing me. I don't deserve it,
but You call me Your beloved child. Help me to
remember others who may feel overlooked or unloved.
Let Your love for them shine through me. Amen.

Confidence

*For I know that my redeemer liveth, and that he shall stand
at the latter day upon the earth: and though after my skin
worms destroy this body, yet in my flesh shall I see God.*

JOB 19:25–26 KJV

Although we experience various difficulties throughout life, we can still look forward to the blessed future we have. No matter what our struggles are, our Lord controls.

Job had no idea what the purpose of his trial was, but he faced his troubles with confidence, knowing that ultimately he would emerge victorious. Too many times we view our own situations with self-pity rather than considering God's strength and trusting that His plan is perfect. What peace God offers when we finally cast our cares on Him and with great conviction declare, "I know that my Redeemer liveth!"

———————

*O great Redeemer, in You I have confidence even when I don't
understand life's trials. Please help me to live victoriously.*

Always Thinking of You

What is man that You are mindful of him,
and the son of man that You visit him?
PSALM 8:4 NKJV

Have you ever wondered what God thinks about? *You* are always on His mind. In all you think and do, He considers you and makes intercession for you. He knows the thoughts and intents of your heart. He understands you like no other person can. He knows your strengths and weaknesses, your darkest fears and highest hopes. He's constantly aware of your feelings and how you interact with or without Him each day.

God is always with you, waiting for you to remember Him—to call on Him for help, for friendship, for anything you need.

Lord, help me to remember You as I go throughout my day. I want to include You in my life and always be thinking of You too. Amen.

Can You Hear Me Now?

But as for me, I watch in hope for the LORD, I wait
for God my Savior; my God will hear me.

MICAH 7:7 NIV

If there's anything more frustrating than waiting for someone who never shows, it's trying to talk to someone who isn't listening. It's as if they have plugged their ears and nothing penetrates. Mothers are well acquainted with this exercise in futility, as are wives, daughters, and sisters. But the Bible tells us that God hears us when we talk to Him. He shows up when we wait for Him. He will not disappoint us.

———————

When I talk, Lord, I know You will listen.
You will never let me down.

Sense of Belonging

"All that the Father gives Me will come to Me, and the one who comes to Me I will by no means cast out."

JOHN 6:37 NKJV

We belong to Christ. When the Father calls us to come to Jesus, we belong to Him. This is an irrevocable transaction. We are His, given to Him by the Father. He does not refuse to save us. He will not refuse to help us. No detail of our lives is unimportant to Him. No matter what happens, He will never let us go. Like the enduring love of a parent—but even more perfect—is the love of Christ for us. He has endured all the temptations and suffered all the pain that we will ever face. He has given His very life for us. We can live peacefully and securely knowing we belong to Him.

Lord Jesus, I confess I often forget I belong to You and how much You love me. Help me to rest in Your everlasting love and care. Amen.

Daily Miracles

"That is why I tell you not to worry about everyday life—whether you have enough food and drink, or enough clothes to wear. Isn't life more than food, and your body more than clothing?"
MATTHEW 6:25 NLT

With our eyes fixed on what we don't have, we often overlook the grace we have already received. God has blessed us in many ways. Our bodies function day after day in amazing ways we take for granted, and life is filled with an abundance of daily miracles. Why do we worry so much about the details when we live in such a vast sea of daily grace?

Father, You are my Provider. You have promised to give me everything I need. Help me to remember this truth and to lose myself in the vast sea of Your amazing grace. Amen.

Lavish and Abundant

*Let them come back to GOD, who is merciful, come
back to our God, who is lavish with forgiveness.*
ISAIAH 55:7 MSG

God's forgiveness is never stingy or grudging. And He never waits
to offer it to us. Instead, it's always there, a lavish, abundant flood
of grace, just waiting for us to turn away from our sin and accept it.

*Lord, when I am consumed by sin, my back is turned to
You. Thank You for Your mercy and lavish forgiveness
that gently turn me toward Your loving arms. Amen.*

From the Inside Out

Take on an entirely new way of life—a God-fashioned life,
a life renewed from the inside and working itself into your
conduct as God accurately reproduces his character in you.
EPHESIANS 4:24 MSG

At the end of a long week, we sometimes feel tired and drained. We need to use feelings like that as wake-up calls, reminders that we need to open ourselves anew to God's Spirit so He can renew us from the inside out. Grace has the power to change our hearts and minds, filling us with new energy to follow Jesus.

———————◆•◆———————

Lord, the world says change comes from the outside. Your
Word says that true transformation comes from the inside.
Meet me there—on the inside—and make me like You. Amen.

Take a Break

"Only in returning to me and resting in me will you be saved."
ISAIAH 30:15 NLT

Some days you try everything you can think of to save yourself, but no matter how hard you try, you fail again and again. You fall on your face and embarrass yourself. You hurt the people around you. You make mistakes, and nothing whatsoever seems to go right. When that happens, it's time to take a break. You need to stop trying so hard. Throw yourself in God's arms. Rest on His grace, knowing He will save you.

———————

Father, sometimes I feel so unsure of myself. Help me to relax, to rest in Your arms, and to remember that You are my good Teacher, my support, and my comfort. Amen.

Our Confidence

*Have no fear of sudden disaster or of the ruin that
overtakes the wicked, for the LORD will be at your
side and will keep your foot from being snared.*

PROVERBS 3:25–26 NIV

Whether our loved ones are in harm's way daily or not, all of us live in a dangerous world. And while we should take physical precautions, our best preparation is spiritual.

When we spend time with God and learn about His love for us and our families, we begin to realize He will give us His grace when we need it. He promises never to leave us, and the more we come to know His love, the more we will rest in that promise.

*God, thank You that You promise Your peace to those who
seek You. Help me to rest in Your love for my family and me.*

Praise Him!

"The LORD is my strength and song, and He has become my salvation. This is my God, and I will praise Him."

EXODUS 15:2 NASB

God makes you strong, He makes you sing with gladness, and He rescues you from sin. These are the gifts of His grace. When He has given you so much, don't you want to give back to Him? Use your strength, your joy, and your freedom to praise Him.

———————

Father, Your Word tells me You have armed me with strength! This is such a gift. Help me to use this strength to honor You. Amen.

Christ-Balance

Jesus caught them off balance with his own test question:
"What do you think about the Christ? Whose son is he?"
MATTHEW 22:41 MSG

Sometimes Christ asks us to find new ways of thinking. . .new ways of living. . .new ways of encountering Him in the world around us. That is not always easy. We don't like to be caught off balance. When our life's equilibrium is shaken, we feel anxious, out of control. But if we rely on Christ, He will pick us up, dust us off and give us the grace to find our balance in Him.

Dear Jesus, sometimes I think I have things all figured out; then You ask a hard question. When I am thrown off balance, steady me with Your truth. Amen.

The Missing Pieces

*Trust the LORD with all your heart, and don't
depend on your own understanding.*

PROVERBS 3:5 NCV

Life is confusing. No matter how hard we try, we can't always make sense of it. We don't like it when that happens, and so we keep trying to determine what's going on, as though we were trying puzzle pieces to fill in a picture we long to see. Sometimes, though, we have to accept that in this life we will never be able to see the entire image. We have to trust God's grace for the missing pieces.

———◆◆———

*Dear Lord, my own understanding is awfully limited,
and yet I still sometimes try to depend on it. Help me
to trust You with 100 percent of my heart. Amen.*

True Beauty

What matters is not your outer appearance—the styling of your hair, the jewelry you wear, the cut of your clothes— but your inner disposition. Cultivate inner beauty, the gentle, gracious kind that God delights in.

1 PETER 3:3-4 MSG

We want to be beautiful. It's a longing that has been in our hearts since we were little girls. As grown-up women, we can become overly worried about our appearance, fretting over whether we measure up to the demanding standards of that little girl who still lives in our hearts. We need to relax in the assurance of God's grace within us. As we allow His Spirit to shine through us, we will find our deepest, truest beauty.

God, instead of focusing on the image I see in my mirror, help me to look into Your eyes for an accurate reflection of the beauty You have instilled in me. Amen.

Outside of Time's Stream

Your throne, O LORD, has stood from time immemorial.
You yourself are from the everlasting past.
PSALM 93:2 NLT

If you think of time as a fast-moving river, then we are creatures caught in its stream. Life keeps slipping away from us like water between our fingers. But God is outside of time's stream. He holds our past safely in His hands, and His grace is permanent and unshakable. His love is the lifesaver to which we cling in the midst of time's wild waves.

———•—•———

God, when I try to understand words like immemorial and everlasting, I am in awe. I cannot begin to comprehend Your bigness. Give me Your perspective. Help me to trust You. Amen.

First Priorities

*For Wisdom is better than all the trappings of wealth;
nothing you could wish for holds a candle to her.*
PROVERBS 8:11 MSG

What do you value most? You may know the answer you are "supposed" to give to that question, but you can tell the real answer by where your time and energy are focused. Do you spend most of your time working for and thinking about money and physical wealth, or do you make wisdom and grace your first priorities?

*Father, if I compare myself too much with others, I can easily
get caught in the trappings of wealth. Instead, turn my focus
to You and help me to make wisdom my goal. Amen.*

Wise Enough to Lead

"To God belong wisdom and power;
counsel and understanding are his."

JOB 12:13 NIV

The word *wisdom* comes from the same root words that have to do with vision, the ability to see into a deeper spiritual reality. Where else can we turn for the grace to see beneath life's surface except to God? Who else can we trust to be strong enough and wise enough to lead us to our eternal home?

———◆◆———

Lord, my vision is far from 20/20. Help me see the
world through Your lens of wisdom. Bestow on me Your
counsel and fill me with Your understanding. Amen.

Heartfelt

For we live by believing and not by seeing.
2 CORINTHIANS 5:7 NLT

The world of science tells us that only what can be seen and measured is truly real. But our hearts know differently. Every day we depend on the things we believe—our faith in God and in our friends and family, our commitment to give ourselves to God and others—and it is these invisible beliefs that give us grace to live.

———•◆•———

Father, my mind is so prone to cling to what is tangible. But my heart is sure that You are as real as the bright shining sun. Fill me with confidence and trust. Amen.

Careful Plans

Without good advice everything goes wrong—
it takes careful planning for things to go right.
PROVERBS 15:22 CEV

The Bible reminds us that when we start a new venture, we should not trust success to come automatically. We need to seek out the advice of those we trust. We need to make careful plans. And most of all, we need to seek God's counsel, praying for the grace and wisdom to do things right.

———————

Father, there are so many opportunities for me to grab hold of. It's tempting to dive in head first. I desperately need Your counsel. Fill me with Your grace and wisdom. Amen.

Amazing Expectations

*Listen to my voice in the morning, LORD. Each
morning I bring my requests to you and wait expectantly.*
PSALM 5:3 NLT

You need to get in the habit of hoping. Instead of getting up in the
morning and sighing as you face another dreary day, practice saying
hello to God as soon as you wake up. Listen for what He wants to
say to your heart. Expect Him to do amazing things each day.

———————

*Good morning, Lord. I can easily forget how necessary it
is to begin my day in sweet communion with You. Tune my
heart's ear to the lovely sound of Your voice. Amen.*

Quiet, Gentle Grace

*"Let me teach you, because I am humble and gentle
at heart, and you will find rest for your souls."*
MATTHEW 11:29 NLT

Sometimes we keep trying to do things on our own, even though
we don't know what we're doing and even though we're exhausted.
And all the while, Jesus waits quietly, ready to show us the way. He
will lead us with quiet, gentle grace, carrying our burdens for us.
We don't have to try so hard. We can finally rest.

———————————

*Jesus, I don't like feeling incompetent and inadequate.
It makes me feel anxious and exhausted. Thank
You for Your gentle teaching and for the strength
You provide. Give me Your rest. Amen.*